The ABC's of
Parent Involvement
in Education

The ABC's of Parent Involvement in Education:
Preparing Your Child for a Lifetime of Success. For information,
write:

National Parents' Day Coalition,
1025 Connecticut, Avenue, N.W., Suite 615,
Washington, D.C. 20036

or

call: (202) 530-0849
fax: (202) 887-6109
E-Mail: npdc@vidtel.com

Cover design by InMind Inc.

Typography and layout by Sam Brown, Photo/Graphics

Publication consultant, Frank Thomasson

Technical assistance, Harlie S. Spencer, III

ISBN 0-9663119-0-6

The ABC's of Parent Involvement in Education: Preparing Your Child for a Lifetime of Success is a compilation of works, tips and information by members, associates and experts affiliated with the National Parents' Day Coalition.

Printed in the United States.

The ABC's of
Parent Involvement
in Education

National Parents' Day Coalition, Washington, D.C.

Acknowledgments

Just as it "takes a village to raise a child," it took a community of associates, friends, and family members to produce this special guide on parent involvement for parents and families.

We extend special thanks to all those who took the time to submit materials, write answers to the questions, review the manuscript, and give suggestions.

No project of this type could happen without the dedication of people who do the typing, reviewing and who provide moral support. Thank you:

Angela Barnes

Suzanne Begin

Louise S. Carey

Michelle Doyle

The Honorable Walter E. Fauntroy

Curtis Hatten

Gywneth Hughes

Houston Council on Alcohol and Drug Abuse

Iris Patten

Virginia Schmidt

Janel Vaughan

Rev. Lee P. Washington, Ph.D.

Yvette Williams

Gladys Wright

Shirley Wright

Finally, there are the children like Perry O'Neal Wright, Kendall, Ashley, Hyojon, Trina, Tasya and Hana who inspire us all.

Dedicated to mothers and fathers, families, guardians, grandparents, aunts, uncles, godparents, stepparents, foster parents, and all those who share in the responsibility of educating and raising a child and who make a lifetime commitment to their children.

Contents

The book is divided into six sections with a table of contents at the beginning of each section.

Section 1 Questions Parents Ask and more. . . about parent involvement, parent involvement initiatives, parent-teacher conferences and homework 2

Section 2 Dads Do Make A Difference! 37

Section 3 Start Right! Tips, information and activities for before birth to pre-K 47

Section 4 Ready To Learn! 70

Section 5 Helping Your Teen To Succeed 107

Section 6 You Are Not Alone! Here you will find resources, Website addresses, and information about organizations and more 135

How to Use this Guide

This guide is interactive. There are checklists, pages for notes, surveys and a parent involvement checkup test. It is inspirational! Throughout the book, you will find short stories, poems and essays from parents and parenting professionals. Topics range from helping a child to learn a new skill, being there for an important event, abuse and to dealing with hate crimes and violence. There are resources, contact information, activities and things to do with your children. Use it daily!

A Word to Parents

From the Publisher:

As a parent, you already have many things that cause anxieties in your daily life, including finances, time, and job pressures. Finding the time to get involved in your child's education adds even more stress. Many surveys have been done to show that usually it is not a lack of interest that keeps parents and families from becoming involved in their children's education, but other barriers and constraints like time, feeling of nothing to contribute, not understanding the system, and feeling intimidated.

This guide is to raise awareness, to energize, and empower parents with ideas and ways that they can overcome these barriers. This book is a tool filled with information, inspiration and ideas. We encourage you to use it as a guide to develop and enhance your involvement in your children's education.

National Parents' Day Coalition

Belinda Rollins
President

Suzanne Begin, Chairperson
National Advisory board

From our Partners:

Hand in Hand, a national initiative, funded by the Mattel Foundation and coordinated by the Institute for Educational leadership, was established to enhance current initiatives and share information about programs that expect, value, and nurture the role families and communities play in children's learning. Hand in Hand has helped bring attention to the broad range of ways cities across the nation have increased parental and community involvement, with particular attention paid to efforts in Birmingham, Chicago, Los Angeles, New York, Philadelphia, Portland, San Antonio, and Tampa.

We are pleased to be a supporter and partner with the National Parents' Day Coalition, WJLA-TV, 7-Eleven Stores, and Appalachia Educational Laboratory in bringing this publication to the Washington area community. We trust that you will find it a helpful tool for your family.

Alfred Ramirez, Director, Hand In Hand:
Parents-Schools-Communities United For Kids

Involving families in their children's learning is getting a lot of attention these days. More than three decades of research validate the importance of family involvement. Contemporary studies have found consistent evidence that when parents encourage children, show interest in children's learning at home, and participate at school, they affect their children's achievement, even after student ability and family socioeconomic status are taken into account.

AEL is pleased to be involved in *The ABC's of Parent Involvement in Education*. We are confident that those of you who use this publication will be better able to be involved in your children's education.

Robert D. Childers, Senior Manager
Appalachia Educational Laboratory

From the Editors:

Let's face it, we all need help in raising our children! No one has all the questions or knows all of the answers. We need each other– the wisdom of the ages, the wisdom of the greater community to succeed.

We, as parents, are to provide our children with the meaning to life to assist them in the discovery of their true identity, and to support them through the years to gain an education, not just to have instruction. More than any other person, organization or system we, as parents, are responsible to help our children learn to think, to use knowledge for the public and private good.

We hope this resource guide will provide you with fingertip information and quicker accessibility for larger questions and issues regarding parent involvement in education.

John W. Robbins
Journalist and father of four

Everyday becomes a test of parenting knowhow. We are constantly bombarded with new and impossible questions. Our instincts are challenged. Our emotions run high. It's important to remember, we all make mistakes and we are most certainly not alone. The most horrific occurrence that happened to you and your child has most likely happened to other families. It's also important to remember that help and assurance are available in many forms, as compiled here in *The ABCs of Parent Involvement in Education.*

Susan Mitgang
Leslie Lombre
The Parent Guide

The most important thing you can do with your child is to enjoy the time you spend learning together. Remember, childhood is not a race to achievement—it should be a journey of discovery, with time to explore the byways. Children learn naturally and eagerly. When you spend some of your valuable time with them, doing learning activities and reading aloud, they learn joyously. As busy as you are, do try to find time to be involved in their education. Nothing you do will give you a bigger payoff.

Patricia Penn
Writer and Editor
Family Connections at AEL

NPDC Advisory Board

QUESTIONS

PARENTS

ASK

About Parent Involvement 2

About Initiatives 7

About Homework 16

About Parent-Teacher Conferences 20

Who's Who in My Child's Education? 23

How Do You Rate? 25

What Really Matters 27
Richard W. Riley
U.S. Secretary of Education

What Will Parents Vote For? 29
National Parenting Association

ABC's of Parent Involvement 32

Q & A

About Parent Involvement

 ## WHAT IS PARENT/FAMILY INVOLVEMENT IN EDUCATION?

"Parent involvement is the participation of parents in every facet of the education and development of children from birth to adulthood, recognizing that parents are the primary influence in their children's lives. Parent involvement takes many forms, including the parents' shared responsibilities in decisions about children's education, health and well-being, as well as the parents' participation in organizations that reflect the community's collaborative aspirations for all children."

The National PTA

 ## WHY IS INVOLVEMENT IMPORTANT?

The research evidence is now beyond dispute. When schools work together with families to support learning, children tend to succeed not just in school, but throughout life. In fact, the most accurate predictor of a student's achievement in school is not income nor social status, but the extent to which that student's family is able to (1) create a home environment that encourages learning, (2) express high (but not unrealistic) expectations for their children's achievement and future careers, and (3) become involved in their children's education at school and in the community.

A. Henderson, National Committee for Citizens in Education

ARE THERE REALLY ANY BENEFITS?

The benefits are many. Students get better grades and achievement test scores, there are fewer discipline problems, lower crime rates, higher graduation rates, less need for special education, happier parents, happier children, stronger families, happier teachers, and better communities just to name a few.

Dr. John H. Wherry, President, The Parent Institute

ARE PARENTS INVOLVED ENOUGH IN SCHOOL?

High school juniors and seniors said in a recent survey that parents are not very involved in preparing their children for school. The company president conducting the survey called it, "an indictment of parents by their own children." They gave parents a "D." Students in the survey responded, only 14% of parents were heavily involved, 44% were somewhat involved, and 30% were rarely or never involved.

Adapted from Family Connections,
Appalachia Educational Laboratory

IF PARENT/FAMILY INVOLVEMENT IS SO IMPORTANT TO LEARNING, WHY ISN'T MORE OF IT HAPPENING?

Although parents and other family members want to do their best to encourage their children's learning, many believe they are not qualified to teach their children. Others struggle with cultural or language barriers. Even without these personal obstacles, families may not know how to become involved with their children's learning at home or at school. Even parents who do know, face resistance from the schools themselves. And all families have the time constraints that come from balancing work and family life. In each of these situations, a partnership between families, schools, community organizations, and/or businesses could help remove the barriers to involvement.

U.S. Department of Education

ARE THERE ANY TIPS FOR A SINGLE MOM WHO KNOWS NOTHING ABOUT SPORTS, BUT WANTS TO BE INVOLVED WITH HER SON?

Refuse to let being a female single parent of a son prevent you from knowing, or him from participating in a sports program. Enroll your youngster in some local team sports program, community or school based. Talk to someone who knows about sports – a relative, friend, co-worker. Read material about sports – books, newspapers, etc. Watch in person and televised events, seeking to increase your own knowledge. Some parents become involved with their young people by being fans and being there, cheering for them. Give of your time.

> Dr. Jerry Semper, Coaching Academy for
> Personal Development, (301) 925-8940.

 ## WHAT ROLE CAN GRANDPARENTS PLAY?

Dr. T. Berry Brazelton encourages grandparents to take their role seriously. He suggests in between visits to fill the gaps with a weekly phone call to the child at a prearranged time. "Encourage each child to share a *news* item with you, something only he or she can reveal. Videotapes are another wonderful way of keeping up with grand children's everyday experiences and milestones. Exchange letters or e-mail and ask for packages of drawings and school work. Your positive feedback helps to build self-esteem." For a free copy of *A Grandparents' Guide for Family Nurturing and Safety* call (800) 638-2772 or visit the website at http://www.cpsc.gov

> U.S. Consumer Product Safety Commission

 ## WHAT ROLE SHOULD PARENTS PLAY IN ACTUAL SCHOOL DECISION MAKING?

There are several approaches to the role of parents in school involvement. In a report published by The Institute for Educational Leadership, the following scenarios were given. They represent the different approaches and provide a framework for meaningful public dialogue. Which school would you prefer in your neighborhood?

• In **Elementary School A,** parents help run the school by serving on a school management council with teachers and the principal. The council decides whom to hire as principal, where to spend the school's money, what to emphasize in the curriculum, and what textbooks and other instructional materials will be used. Parents are elected to the council by other parents from the school and have as many votes on the council as the professional educators.

- In **Elementary School B,** parents are asked to support their children's education at home, in close cooperation with the school. Parents are expected to limit the amount of television their kids watch, check their homework regularly, make sure their kids have the space and quiet they need to study effectively, and set high expectations for learning. Finally parents are asked to support the teachers and principals on discipline and grading policies.

- **In Elementary School C,** parents are encouraged to attend parent/ teacher conferences and open houses and to help with school fundraising. But with so many broken homes, social problems, and people working extra jobs, the school cannot count on parents to be actively involved. Therefore, the school must take on many of the roles once filled by parents. This might include serving breakfast as well as lunch, teachers getting more involved in the home life of their students, mentor programs bringing in adult role models, and social workers helping kids in need.

Individuals or organizations interested in learning more about IEL's and Public Agenda's Public Engagement Program should contact Mrs. Jacqueline P. Danzberger, Director of Governance Programs at (202) 822-8405, ext. 54 or e-mail danzberg@iel.org.

 WHERE CAN PARENTS GET HELP WITH PARENT INVOLVEMENT TECHNIQUES AND SKILLS?

The National Council of Jewish Women, Center for the Child identified and researched promising parent involvement programs for school districts around the country. Here are a few of the curriculum models and workshops highlighted in the report. For a complete list and Dissemination Kit containing Project Overview, Literature Review, School Superintendents' Survey, Parent, Teacher, and School Principal Focus Group findings, contact the NCJW, 53 West 23rd Street, 6th Floor, New York, N.Y. 10010, Telephone: (212) 645-4048. Or visit their website at http://www.ncjw.org

Bowdoin Method I/II
Parents learn a variety of parent involvement lessons, cognitive skills, methods of how children learn, and emotional and social needs of children.

Contact: Virginia Schmidt, Webster's International Inc.
(800) 727-6833

MegaSkills
Workshops help parents learn how to use "recipes" of home learning activities with their child. Focuses on life skills for academic achievement and emotional growth.

Contact: Dr. Dorothy Rich, Home School Institute, (202) 466-3633

Parents on Board
Workshops help parents learn techniques on how to help children succeed in school.

Contact: Karen Sullivan, Active Parenting Press, (800) 825-0060

Parents Assuring Student Success (PASS)
This book is available at a cost of $21.95. It provides information and resources to help parents.

Contact: Susan Dunkar, National Educational Service, (800) 733-6786

**Studying at Home/Reading
at Home**
Workshops to assist parents in helping their child study and read.

Contact: Sam Redding, Academic Development Institute,
(800) 759-1495

Q & A

About Initiatives

 WHAT IS TITLE I, IMPROVING AMERICA'S SCHOOLS ACT OF 1994?

Title I is the largest federal aid program for elementary, middle, and high schools. Through Title I, the federal government gives money to school districts around the country based on the number of low-income families in each district. Each district uses Title I money for extra educational services for children who are behind in school. We formerly knew it as Chapter I. The new Title I is different.

 WHICH STUDENTS CAN GET TITLE I HELP?

Each school community decides which students are most in need of Title I services. Schools where more than half of all students are low-income can operate a school-wide Title I project.

 HOW CAN TITLE I HELP ME AS A PARENT?

Title I money can be used for many types of parent involvement activities including family literacy, parent meetings and training, transportation and child care so that parents can attend school activities or volunteer in the classroom.

What Is a "Compact For Learning?"

A "compact" is a written statement of what parents and schools are committed to do to help students achieve. It is a commitment to sharing responsibility for student learning and an action plan for family–school–community partnerships to help children get a high–quality education. Each school receiving Title I funds also must have a compact.

 What is The Purpose of a Compact and How Can I Use It?

The compact lists the specific duties of school staff and parents. With a compact, everybody knows what they are supposed to do. It helps everyone keep on track in support of students. You can use the compact as a kind of job description. It lists the things that you can do to support your child's progress at school. You also can use the compact to make sure the school is doing its job of teaching your child what he or she needs to know in order to achieve in life and to meet the expected standards. For more information call (202) 260-0965 or to receive a free brochure about compacts call (703) 528-3588, (800) 925-3223 or (800) USA-LEARN.

 How Can We Learn More About Title I?

To get a copy of Improving America's School Act of 1994, contact the U.S. Senate Document Room, telephone (202) 224-7701, fax: (202) 228-2815. To get a free brochure about Title I, call (703) 528-3588 or toll free at (800) 925-3223.

 What Is a School Parent Involvement Policy?

A parent involvement policy explains how the school district or the school itself supports the important role of parents in the education of their children. Every school district which receives Title I money must have a parent involvement policy. Every school in the district receiving Title I money also must have a policy.

How Is The Parent Involvement Policy Developed?

The process that is used to develop the policy and put it into action will vary. However, each district and each school is required to involve parents in the process. It also is required to give a copy of the policy to parents of every child in Title I.

 ### Where Can We Find More Information About Parent Involvement Policies?

Your child's teacher should be able to provide you with more information. Other people who should be able to answer your questions include the school's principal, the school's Title I director, or the superintendent of schools. To obtain a free brochure about parent involvement policies, call (703) 528-3588 or (800) 925-3223.

 ### What Is Provided To Families Of Students With Disabilities?

The United States Department of Education's Office of Special Education and Rehabilitative Services (OSERS), through its Office of Special Education Programs (OSEP), helps states carry out their responsibilities to provide to all students with disabilities a free, appropriate public education in the least restrictive environment. These responsibilities are spelled out in the Individuals with Disabilities Education Act (IDEA).

For more information contact the Office of Special Education and Rehabilitative Services, U.S. Department of Education, 330 C Street, SW, Washington, D.C. 20202. Telephone: (202) 205-5507 or visit on the internet at http://www.ed.gov/offices/OSERS/

 ### What Is The "Hope Scholarship" Tax Credit For Students Starting College?

The "Hope Scholarship" tax credit helps make the first two years of college or vocational school universally available. Students will receive a 100% tax credit for the first $1,000 of tuition and required fees and a 50% credit on the second $1,000. This credit is available for tuition and required fees less grants, scholarships, and other tax-free educational assistance and will be available for payments made after December 31, 1997 for college enrollment after that date. A high school senior going into his or her freshman year of college in September, 1998, for example, could be eligible for as much as a $1,500 HOPE tax credit.

 ## WHO BENEFITS FROM THE "LIFETIME LEARNING" TAX CREDIT?

This tax credit is targeted to adults who want to go back to school, change careers, or take a course or two to upgrade their skills and to college juniors, seniors, graduate and professional degree students. A family will receive a 20% tax credit for the first $5,000 of tuition and required fees paid each year through 2002, and for the first $10,000 thereafter. Just like the "HOPE Scholarship" tax credit, the Lifetime Learning tax credit is available for tuition and required fees less grants, scholarships, and other tax–free educational assistance; families may claim the credit for amounts paid on or after July 1, 1998 for college or vocational school enrollment beginning on or after July 1, 1998. For more information visit http://www.ed.gov/inits/hope/97918tax.html

 ## WHAT IS AVAILABLE FOR STUDENTS WHO ARE NOT COLLEGE BOUND?

The School-to-Work Opportunities Act, broadens educational, career and economic opportunities for students in high school, including creating pathways for those not immediately bound for four year colleges and for the many young people who cannot see the relevance of what they're doing in the classrooms to the world of work, and thus get bored and tune out. When the barrier between academic learning and vocational education is broken, when work-based learning and school-based learning are linked, these students not only stay in school, but they become engaged in learning and do better and continue on to college.

What is Goals 2000: Educate America Act?

Goals 2000 is the U.S. Department of Education's flagship program to help parents, teachers, and community leaders improve their own schools by raising academic standards; addressing safety, discipline, and basic skills; attracting and training better teachers; and strengthening parent involvement. For more information, telephone your state education department or the U.S. Department of Education at (800) USA-LEARN

GOALS 2000

GOAL 1: READY TO LEARN
By the year 2000, all children in America will start school ready to learn.

GOAL 2: SCHOOL COMPLETION
By the year 2000, the high school graduation rate will increase to at least 90 percent.

GOAL 3: STUDENT ACHIEVEMENT AND CITIZENSHIP
By the year 2000, all students will leave grades 4, 8, and 12 having demonstrated competency over challenging subject matter including English, mathematics, science, foreign languages, civics and government, economics, arts, history and geography, and every school in America will ensure that all students learn to use their minds well, so they may be prepared for responsible citizenship, further learning, and productive employment in our nation's modern economy.

GOAL 4: TEACHER EDUCATION AND PROFESSIONAL DEVELOPMENT
By the year 2000, the nation's teaching force will have access to programs for the continued improvement of their professional skills and the opportunity to acquire the knowledge and skills needed to instruct and prepare all American students for the next century.

GOAL 5: MATHEMATICS AND SCIENCE
By the year 2000, United States students will be first in the world in mathematics and science achievement.

GOAL 6: ADULT LITERACY AND LIFELONG LEARNING
By the year 2000, every adult American will be literate and will possess the knowledge and skills necessary to compete in a global economy and exercise the rights and responsibilities of citizenship.

GOAL 7: SAFE, DISCIPLINED, AND ALCOHOL-AND DRUG-FREE SCHOOLS
By the year 2000, every school in the United States will be free of drugs, violence, and the unauthorized presence of firearms and alcohol and will offer a disciplined environment conducive to learning.

GOAL 8: PARENTAL PARTICIPATION
By the year 2000, every school will promote partnerships that will increase parental involvement and participation in promoting the social, emotional, and academic growth of children.

For Your Involvement!

Special Days and Observances

Take Our Parents to School (TOPS) Week

Join Hand in Hand: Parents-Schools-Communities United for Kids for our annual **Take Our Parents to School (TOPS) Week**. Scheduled to coincide with American Education Week, **November 15-21**, 1998, TOPS Week will: highlight opportunities for parents and schools to exchange and share information, reach out to parents and family members who are not currently involved in their children's education at school by offering a range of opportunities to participate, support organizations who are currently active in children's schools and in community-parent involvement activities, expand the range of opportunities for the involvement of businesses and other community groups to more actively support parents and schools, and provide an environment for continuing commitment and relationship-building activities. For more information contact Hand in Hand at (202) 882-8405 ext. 25 or toll free (800) 953–HAND.

National Parent Involvement Day

This year Hand in Hand and the National Parents' Day Coalition will join efforts to establish the first day of Take Our Parents To School Week and National Education Week as **National Parent Involvement Day.** The day is modeled after the excellent example of the Texas Education Agency, Parent Involvement and Community Empowerment Unit. Its Director, Albert L. Black has successfully spearheaded an annual observance every November 12th with such activities as a state Parent Involvement Conference, publication of a training manual in conjunction with the Texas PTA, and a series of broadcast on the T-Star Satellite.

You are invited to join the campaign. Call Hand in Hand at (202) 822–8405 ext. 25 or toll free (800) 953–HAND for more information about how you can get involved.

National African-American Parent Involvement Day

Joseph Dulin, principal at Ann Arbor, Michigan's Robert Clemente High School is the founder of National African-American Parent Involvement Day (NAAPID). Dulin has always stressed the importance of parental involvement within the school, but he also felt that African-American parents have tended to stay way. He suspected that African-American parents' own experiences had been negative. Inspired by the Million Man March and challenged to go back home to do something positive for the African-American community, the seed for NAAPID was born. It is celebrated annually on the second Monday in February during Black History Month.

National Parents' Day – A Day To Honor Parents

The fourth Sunday in July

Parents' Day is a national day to honor parents. It is a day designated "to uplift and support the important role of parents in the rearing of their children." President Clinton signed the bill into law designating the fourth Sunday in July as Parents' Day in October, 1994 after unanimous approval in the House and Senate.

> "Resolved by the Senate and House of Representatives of the United States of America in the Congress assembled, That the fourth Sunday of every July shall be established as "Parents' Day" to be recognized as a recurring, perennial day of commemoration.
>
> SEC,2. RECOGNITION.
>
> All private citizens, organizations, and governmental and legislative bodies at the local, State, and Federal level are encouraged to recognize Parents' Day through proclamations, activities, and educational efforts in furtherance of recognizing, uplifting, and supporting the role of parents in the rearing of their children."

What You Can Do:

- Host or sponsor a Parents' Day observance in your school, community, business or place of worship.

- Sponsor an essay contest on responsible parenting, parent involvement or about values and tradition by having the participants write about a valuable lesson or habit that they learned or remember from their parent or parenting figure.

- Recognize outstanding parents in your community.

- Recognize and support businesses who support workplace policies in support of families.

- Spend time with your children.

- Become a member of the National Parents' Day Coalition and support efforts to promote responsible parenting and parent involvement.

For more information call (202) 530-0849.

Q & A

About

Homework

 WHY IS THERE A NEED FOR HOMEWORK?

Homework can help your child learn and can help you be involved in their education. When you show an interest in your child's school work, an important lesson is taught–that learning can be fun and is worth the effort. Children who do more homework, on average, do better in school. And, as children move up through the grades, homework becomes even more important to school success.

Teachers assign homework for many reasons. It can help children:

* practice what they have learned in school;

* get ready for the next day's class;

* use resources, such as libraries and encyclopedias; and

* learn things they don't have time to learn in school.

Homework can also help children learn good habits and attitudes. It can teach children to work by themselves and encourage discipline and responsibility.

What Do We Do When Our Child Tries to Avoid Doing Home Work?

Here are practical, tested ways from Dr. Dorothy Rich's MegaSkills related book, *What Do We Say? What Do We Do? (Forge Books, 1997)*

When your child asks: *"Homework is awful. Why do I have to do it?"*

Try these responses: *"To tell you the truth, I didn't always enjoy my homework when I was in school either. I made some of the same fuss you are making."*

"It doesn't always take a lot of time. I know that it's not always fun, but it is your job."

 ## How Much Time Should my Child Spend on Homework?

According to some researchers, two ways to increase opportunities for students to learn are to (1) increase the amount of time students have to learn and (2) to expand the amount of content they receive. Homework assignments may foster both these goals.

According to statements by the National PTA and the National Education Association (NEA), the following amounts of homework are recommended:

From kindergarten to third grade, no more than 20 minutes per day.

From fourth to sixth grade, 20 to 40 minutes per day.

From seventh to twelfth grade, the recommended amount of time varies according to the type and number of subjects a student is taking. In general, college-bound students receive lengthier and more involved homework than students preparing to enter the workforce immediately after graduation.

 ## What Can We Do to Ensure a Stress-free Environment For Doing Homework?

Children should be given time to rest and play when they come home from school. Help your child establish a regular time to do homework. If there is no homework assignment, let them read a book, review or spend time studying. You can help by following these suggestions.

1. Have a quiet place for your child to study. Remember, television, radio and CD's don't mix with homework.

2. Have a place for all materials usually needed for homework.

3. Help your children by being available to assist with questions. But remember, it is their homework, not yours!

4. Encourage your child to complete homework neatly and accurately.

5. Keep lines of communications open with the school.

6. Set a good example during study time. Try reading. Do not watch television or be on the phone.

 ## How Can we Give Guidance Without Doing the Homework Ourselves?

The basic rule in helping with homework is, "don't do the assignment yourself. It's not your homework–it's your child's." Here are some things you can do to give guidance:

- **Figure out how your child learns best.** Knowing this makes it easier for you to help your child. For example, if your child learns things best when he can see them, draw a picture or a chart to help with some assignments. But if your child learns best when she can handle things, an apple cut four ways can help her learn fractions. If you've never thought about this learning style, observe your child. Check with the teacher if you aren't sure.

- **Encourage good study habits.** See that your child schedules enough time for assignments and makes his own practice tests at home before a test. When a big research report is coming up, encourage her to use the library, read more than is necessary and not to procrastinate.

- **Talk about assignments and ask questions**. This helps your child think through an assignment and break it into small, workable parts. For example, ask if she understands the assignment, whether she needs help with the work, and if her answer makes sense to her.

- **Give praise.** People of all ages like to be told when they have done a good job. Give helpful criticism when your child hasn't done his best work, so he can improve.

- **Communicate.** Talk with someone at school if problems come up. If homework problems do arise, everyone needs to work together to resolve them–the parents, students, teachers, and the school. Call or meet with the teacher if your child refuses to do assignments, or if you or your child can't understand the instructions, or if you can't help your child get organized to do the assignments. Remember, it takes a village to raise a child.

 ## WHAT IS THE BEST WAY TO HELP WITH THE LONG TERM ASSIGNMENTS?

It is advisable to have a monthly calendar on which long term assignments can be written. Sit down with your child and read over the directions or discuss the nature of the assignment. Make a list of the steps necessary to complete the assignment. Draw up a time line. Each subtask should have a due date attached to it and it should be written on the monthly calendar. Care should be taken to ensure that adequate time is available for each step.

This information was taken from *Helping Your Child with Homework,* U.S. Department of Education. To find out what's available and how to order, request a free catalog from the Consumer Information Catalog, Pueblo, Colorado 81009.

 ## WHERE CAN PARENTS FIND OUT MORE ABOUT HOMEWORK GUIDELINES?

ERIC Clearinghouse on Elementary and Early Childhood Education
University of Illinois at Urbana-Champaign
Children's Research Center
51 Gerty Drive, Champaign, IL 61820–7469
(217) 333-1386

National Education Association
1201 16th Street, NW, Washington, DC 20036
(202) 822-7214

The National PTA
700 North Rush Street, Chicago, IL 60611-2571
(312) 787-0977

Q & A

About Parent-Teacher Conferences

 ### What Should We Expect at The Meeting?

The parent-teacher conference can be a bit intimidating, especially if it's your first one or your first with a new teacher. Remember that a teacher is probably as nervous about meeting you as you are about meeting him or her. Even former teachers are often nervous when they're placed in a parent role.

Before you go, talk about the upcoming conference with your child. Ask if there are any subjects that they want you to discuss with the teacher.

Take a "what can we do" and "how can I help" attitude if the teacher brings up a problem or even if your child seems to be doing alright. You can help your child, but you can't make him or her into a perfect child nor a super student.

Vicki Lansky
Columnist, *Family Circle Magazine*

WHAT TYPES OF QUESTIONS SHOULD WE ASK?

It is a very good idea to make a list of questions. Basic topics should cover achievement, behavior, peer relationships, and self-esteem. You also may wish to discuss methods of discipline. Here are some suggestions of questions.

1. How is our child doing in reading? In math? In science?

2. How are the work habits? Is work finished on time?

3. Is homework turned in on time?

4. Does my child need help in a special area?

 ## WHAT TYPES OF THINGS SHOULD WE SHARE WITH THE TEACHER?

It helps when the teacher knows of any changes or special needs that your child may have. Examples of things that may be helpful for the teacher to know include:

- Anything that has happened recently which may cause a shift in behavior or performance.

- Health problems your child has or previously had, including medications.

- Responsibilities your child has at home.

- Your child's out of school activities and friends.

 ## WHAT ARE MY RIGHTS TO MY CHILD'S RECORDS?

There is a law governing your rights to your child's records. The Family Education Rights and Privacy Act, also known as the "Buckley Amendment," was passed by Congress in 1974. The legislation guarantees the following parent rights to access of school records:

- The right of access to all information and material kept by the school about your child, regardless of format or location of such material.

- The right to challenge and correct information included in such material.

- The right to determine who, other than school district personnel has the right to access your child's records.

You should review your child's records at least once each year. In addition it is a good idea to review records before a parent-teacher conference, following discipline or academic problems, and whenever your child changes grades, schools, or school districts.

Across the country, parents are suing and fighting in court over their rights to information concerning their children's education. There is a new bill in congress that would expand on the Buckley Act. The new measure would bolster parents' rights and penalize noncompliant schools by withholding federal money.

The measure would guarantee access to such curricula-related materials as textbooks, films, manuals and audiovisual materials. Parents would have the right to see the tests their children take, except standardized achievement and copyright tests. It would require schools to obtain parental consent before students undergo medical, psychological or psychiatric examination or treatment at school.

Rep. Todd Tiahrt, R-Kansas is a sponsor of the new bill. The National PTA is not in favor of the bill and believes that parental rights legislation could interfere with child abuse laws and school discipline codes.

 ## WHAT ARE PARENT-TEACHER ASSOCIATIONS DOING TO MEET THE NEEDS OF TODAY'S PARENTS?

There are reports from across the country that parent-teacher associations and organizations are changing to meet the needs of parents. Meetings are being held in community centers, at places of employment and in public facilities during times that are more convenient for parents. Parents and family members are encouraged to discuss ideas and suggestions at local parent-teacher conferences.

Who's Who in My Child's Education

School officials are in their jobs to provide the best education for all the students. It is helpful to them when parents and other citizens share ideas, concerns and questions about the school. Here is a chart to assist you in keeping track of school officials who help in your child's education.

Local School Board

School board members are elected by the public. Find out who your school board members are, how they are elected, and where they stand on important issues. School board members bring an interest in education, a concern for children, a knowledge of their community, a sense of fairness and a great deal of common sense to their positions. The local school board approves the school budget, oversees operations of the school district, and hires and fires the superintendent. Call the school district administration office to obtain the names of your school board members and their contact information.

Local Board Member's Name	Telephone Number	E-Mail

School Superintendent

The superintendent oversees all schools in the district and is responsible for local decisions relating to curriculum, transportation, testing, school schedule and personnel.

Superintendent's Name and Address	Telephone Number	E-Mail

Principal

The principal is responsible for a campus. He/she works with the site-based decision-making committee or team to decide the management direction of the school. While the committee makes recommendations, the principal makes the final decisions based upon his/her legal requirements as administrator of the school.

Principal's Name	Telephone Number	E-Mail

In larger schools, the principal may have one or more assistant principals.

Assistant Principal's Name	Telephone Number	E-Mail

Site-Based Decision-Making Committee/Team

Parent Representative's Name	Telephone Number	E-Mail

Guidance Counselor

The school counselor helps students with personal as well as educational problems and can sometimes be the first contact for families in need of counseling or social services.

School Counselor's Name	Telephone Number	E-Mail

Nurse

The school nurse looks after the health needs of the children. The nurse can provide valuable health information and can also act as a first contact for families in need of counseling or social services.

Nurse's Name	Telephone Number	E-Mail

Adapted from the Texas Education Agency

PARENT INVOLVEMENT CHECKUP
How Do You Rate?

Here are some examples of how you can be involved. Rate your involvement as you see it. If there are two adults in the household, combine their ratings and come up with one number. Rate 1-5, with "1" being low or not true, and "5" being high and true.

✦ Know my children's teachers by name:

1_____ 2_____ 3_____ 4_____ 5_____

✦ Know my children's class schedule:

1_____ 2_____ 3_____ 4_____ 5_____

✦ Attend conferences scheduled to give me information about my children:

1_____ 2_____ 3_____ 4_____ 5_____

✦ Initiate contact with the teachers about my children:

1_____ 2_____ 3_____ 4_____ 5_____

✦ Follow-up on messages which the teacher sends me about my children or the school:

1_____ 2_____ 3_____ 4_____ 5_____

✦ Attend school functions which involve my children:

1_____ 2_____ 3_____ 4_____ 5_____

✦ Attend PTA or other parent-teacher meetings:

1_____ 2_____ 3_____ 4_____ 5_____

✦   Try to help my children in a positive way with their homework:

   1_____ 2_____ 3_____ 4_____ 5_____

✦   Look over and express concern for my children's work which they
    bring home:

   1_____ 2_____ 3_____ 4_____ 5_____

✦   Try to send my children to school clean, rested and well fed:

   1_____ 2_____ 3_____ 4_____ 5_____

✦   Spend some time in my children's classrooms as a volunteer:

   1_____ 2_____ 3_____ 4_____ 5_____

✦   Take my children to the library and to other places which help in
    educating them:

   1_____ 2_____ 3_____ 4_____ 5_____

Now let's add up the scores:

48-60   You're doing super.
27-47   Good effort. You really are trying.
15-26   Needs attention.
0-14   Really needs attention. But there is always hope.

My notes and comments for things that I want to do or change.

_____

_____

_____

_____

_____

_____

                                   Adapted from the Arkansas PTA

United States Secretary of Education Richard W. Riley has made improvement of the nation's schools his number one priority. Throughout his tenure as Secretary of Education, he has emphasized that family involvement in education is one of the keys to improving education. Following is an excerpt from a recent speech by Secretary Riley that looks at American education and the consensus of the nation to make its improvement a national priority. Meaningful family involvement will come from an understanding of these issues and a commitment to act upon them in every school and local community across the country.

WHAT REALLY MATTERS IN AMERICAN EDUCATION

Excerpts from a speech by United States Education
Secretary Richard W. Riley
Given at the National Press Club, September 23, 1997

A new American consensus has now developed about how to improve education. It has taken us over a decade since Ted Bell issued his report, *A Nation at Risk*, to develop this consensus, but everywhere I go I see the core elements of this consensus being put in place.

There is a growing emphasis on early childhood and the importance of pre-k and kindergarten for all children. A second element is a commitment to high standards linked to challenging assessments. The American people recognize that progress is only going to happen if we make sure that every child has mastered the basics once and for all. That's the third element: a clear focus on the fundamentals.

As I travel around the country, I see four other elements to this new education consensus falling into place. These include a stronger focus on more parental involvement; teacher quality; a greater investment in technology; and growing recognition—even among young people—that taking the tough core courses pays off.

The new American consensus on how to improve education is a pragmatic, mainstream consensus, and we are starting to see steady and positive results. Math and science scores have been rising for a decade. SAT scores are up, particularly in math, and ACT scores have gone up in four of the last five years. And one-third of this year's college freshmen took advanced placement courses.

Public education is beginning to improve. We are not where we want to be, but we are headed in the right direction. This is why we need to stay focused on what really matters. I believe that if we focus in on what we agree on and what really matters rather than on what divides us—we can make the next ten years the 'golden era' of American education. The American people have made the improvement of public education a national priority. We know how to fix our schools. Now is the time to roll up our sleeves and get it done.

What Will Parents Vote For?

The National Parenting Association (NPA) commissioned independent pollsters Penn & Shoen to conduct a survey of 500 mothers and fathers. The results are revealing. Contrary to conventional wisdom it turns out that there is real unity across race, class and gender. Blue collar and professional parents, African-American and white parents share a set of urgent concerns and are ready to rally around a common agenda. In addition, there is a tremendous focus on practical rather than ideological issues.

Mothers and fathers agree on what issues matter most to them. Their central concerns revolve around economic pressure and a resultant family time famine. Parents are under enormous stress, struggling to balance their work and family obligations. They think it's high time the government, employers and school changed the rules to recognize that we are now a nation of working parents. An overwhelming 82% of parents say they have a tougher time balancing work and being a parent than their own parents did.

Greater flexibility on the job:

- Ninety percent of parents favor tax incentives to encourage employers to adopt family-friendly policies like benefits for part-time workers and flextime.

- Eighty-seven percent of parents favor a law ensuring 24 hours or 3 days paid leave annually for meeting family needs, like parent-teacher conferences or taking a child to the doctor.

- Seventy-nine percent favor letting workers take time off instead of extra pay for overtime and nearly as many, 71%, would like employees to be able to trade two weeks pay for an extra two weeks vacation.

- Seventy-six percent support legislation requiring medium and large companies to offer up to 12 weeks of paid leave following childbirth or adoption.

Longer school days:

Seventy-five percent of parents would like schools to be kept open longer for classes, supervised homework or activities, to better match the typical day.

Relief from the economic burdens of child-rearing:

- Parents believe that, like in other developed countries, the high cost of raising the next generation —who will, after all, insure the nations' future competitiveness and pay our social security bill — should not be wholly a private burden. By overwhelming margins, parents want tax breaks to help make education affordable—from preschool through college.

- Ninety-four percent of parents favor federal tax credits or deductions to help pay for college for families earning under $100,000.

- State and local sales taxes eliminated on children's necessities, like diapers, car seats and school supplies (favored by 82%). The income tax dependent exemption tripled for children in families with annual incomes under $100,000 (favored by 82%)

Tougher gun control:

Keeping their children safe from violence, crime and drugs are the number one worries of parents. Eighty-nine percent support legislation requiring gun makers to install trigger locks or safety devices to make it harder for kids to fire guns. A stunning majority of parents (53%), would go much further, banning handguns completely.

Quality public schools:

This was spontaneously mentioned by parents as their single concern for their children, after violence and drugs.

Less economic pressure, enchanced workplace flexibility and renewed respect for the job of parenting would enable more parents to give more and better time to their children-either through working fewer more flexible hours, or taking a chunk of time out of the labor market entirely. Mothers and fathers know that "home alone" children do not do well and that parental attention and supervision is enormously important in the raising of well-adjusted children. Their instincts are borne out by the data. A recent study shows that 60% of school achievement is determined by parental involvement.

This new survey tells us that across race, gender and class, parents have the potential of uniting behind a powerful agenda that centers on solving the family time famine. And if America's 62 million mothers and fathers were to unite they would constitute an extremely potent political force.

Borrowing a page from seniors, 89% of parents surveyed thought an organization, like AARP, that is a voice for parents in the public arena would be a good idea. Such an organization might finally ensure that the voices of mothers and fathers are heard in the corridors of power and confer new political clout on families with children.

Cornel West, Professor of African-American Studies at Harvard University and author of *Race Matters*, and Sylvia Ann Hewlett, founding President of the National Parenting Association and author of *When the Bough Breaks: The Cost of Neglecting Our Children*, are co-authors of the forthcoming book, *The War Against Parents* (Houghton Mifflin, Spring 1998) Nancy Rankin is Project Director of the National Parenting Association. All are parents.

The ABC's of Parent Involvement

A... affectionate and caring parents have winning children.

B...build up your children's confidence.

C...cooperate with others who work and care for your children.

D...direct your children's attention to improve listening and speaking skills.

E...establish rules and stick by them. Be consistent!

F...forget about comparing one child to another child.

G...govern with discipline at home, in the community and at school.

H...help your child to know when to say no! Peer pressure is dangerous.

I...institute regular visits to places of interest: libraries, parks, museums, etc.

J...join your child in play time with fun and games.

K...keep lines of communication open.

L...let your child develop interest and hobbies of his own liking.

M...mother, but don't smother your child!

N...never give up on your child!

O...open every possible door of help for your child, it will always be remembered.

P...patience and positive attitudes are positive traits for parents.

Q...quiet children should be observed carefully, they may be insecure, calling out for help or may just be good children.

R...read to your child from cradle to adulthood.

S...socialize with your child and his/her friends. Know who they are.

T...teach your child the difference between right and wrong.

U...utilize your time and your child's wisely; try to follow a routine.

V...visit your child's school often; know the teachers.

W...watch your vocabulary; negative words are easily learned by children.

X...x-ray yourself. Are your actions and attitudes helping your child to become a good student and solid citizen in the community?

Y... you are the most important person in your children's lives; let them know you love them.

Z...zero in on your child's life and live zealously!

Judy Cato, Title I Parent Involvement Manual,Tampa Florida,
"Hand In Hand" Coordinator

National Network of Partnership Schools

Schools, districts, and state departments of education are invited to join the National Network of Partnership Schools at Johns Hopkins University to obtain assistance in implementing permanent and positive programs of school-family-community partnership. Schools are guided to use an action team approach and a research-based framework of six major types of involvement. Each school tailors plans and practices to the needs and interests of its students, parents, and teachers. District and state leaders are helped to organize their leadership activities to assist all schools to conduct this work.

There are no membership fees, but states, districts, and schools must agree to a few requirements for adequate staff, budgets, supports for good work, and communication with the Network. The Center provides members with a handbook, certificate, optional annual training workshops at Johns Hopkins, semi-annual newsletters, phone, e-mail, and website assistance, and annual research and evaluation activities.

For an invitation and membership form, or list of related publications, write to: Dr. Joyce Epstein, Director, National Network of Partnership Schools, Center on School, Family, and Community Partnerships, Johns Hopkins University/CRESPAR, 3505 North Charles Street, Baltimore, Maryland 21218: To contact the Center, tel: (410) 525-8818; fax: (410) 516-8890 or use the Network's website: www.csos.jhu.ed

notes

DADS DO MAKE A DIFFERENCE!

**Fathers' Involvement Makes for Children's
  Academic Success** 38
Partnership For Family Involvement
  In Education, U.S. Department of Education

The Incident 39
Neil Tift, Fathers' Resource Center

Out of the Cold 41
John Reardon, Elementary School Principal
  and Author

Uniting Fathers, Children, and Schools 43
Jeffry Jeanetta-Wark, MA.,LICSW
  Fathers' Resource Center

Fathers' Involvement Makes for Children's Academic Success

Fathers' Involvement in Their Children's Schools, a report released by Vice President Al Gore and U.S. Secretary Richard W. Riley highlights the link between family involvement in education and children's academic success.

A key finding was that fathers and mothers are more likely to be involved in their children's education when schools welcome family involvement. Parental involvement was also higher when the school provided a safe, disciplined, learning environment and when teachers and students respected each other.

The report also found that, while having one parent actively involved in a child's education is important, having both parents involved strengthened a child's chances for academic success. Data for the report were collected from a nationally representative sample of almost 17,000 parents and/or guardians of different racial-ethnic and socioeconomic backgrounds with students in kindergarten through twelfth grade.

Key findings of the report:

- Children are more likely to get mostly A's, and less likely to repeat a grade, if their fathers are involved in their schools.

- Children do better in school when their fathers are involved, regardless of whether their fathers live with them or whether their mothers are also involved.

- Single fathers are far more likely to be involved in their children's schools than fathers in two-parent families.

- The relationships between fathers' involvement and children's success in school are important, regardless of income, race-ethnicity, or the parents' education.

Reprinted from *Community Update*, Partnership for Family Involvement in Education, U.S. Department of Education. To obtain free copies of the report, call The National Library of Education at (800) 424–1616, or visit http://nces.ed.gov/pubs98/fathers/index.html

The Incident

I walked in our front door ready to question my son about some trivial transgression that I thought required immediate attention. He was sitting on the couch holding an ice bag to his head. Zach didn't look like the usual jovial, man-boy I've been struggling to raise for 17 years. Then I saw why.

His left eye was closed and badly bruised, his left ear was mangled, his lips three times their usual size, two front teeth were dislodged, his nose was a shape I'd never seen before, his face, neck and arms were bloodied and scarred, and his breathing was labored.

My initial reaction was to run to him and hold him to try to make it all better, but I couldn't find any place to touch that wouldn't seem to hurt him even more. He had been jumped, beaten, kicked and brutalized because he was white and alone at night on a busy street in South Minneapolis. I struggled to comfort him and to offer the loving response that any caring parent naturally offers to their battered child.

I also became aware of the struggle of emotions within me. Rage, frustrations, pity, anger, sadness and revenge came to mind. Why Zach? One of the most tolerant and accepting kids I know. Why Zach? Who although he is six feet and two inches tall, and a big strong kid, is very gentle, and enjoys baby-sitting his little brothers. His favorite job is working summers at a camp for children with autism. Why Zach? Someone who is so good and decent and caring. Then I realized this implies that terrible things should only happen to bad and indecent people.

I felt truly fortunate that I have a circle of healthy men friends to talk with. I called one of them Sunday and met another on Monday.

I began to process some of the reactions that were seething within. As I sorted some of these through, talked, cried, and wondered aloud, I came–stumbled really–to several conclusions. Random acts of violence are just that–random.

Stranger-to-stranger crime selects those who look vulnerable, not those who don't like my son. They probably weren't attacking him because of the individual he was, but because he was there, and alone, not different from them.

The racial thing really bothered me. We shared our home with a black family for five months until recently. Half of the teenagers coming to wish Zach a speedy recovery were adolescent boys of all races. My grandson is black. I wasn't worried that our family would all of a sudden turn racist. But, I was having trouble coping with the potential repercussions of this incident.

Just as I was there to soothe Zach's physical pain, I had to be ready to help with the emotional healing. I came to realize that more than race, neighborhood, or age it was really a gender thing. What we were teaching our boys and men about masculinity, virility, coming of age, self-image, anger and fitting in?

We glorify men who tell us to settle everything through the use of martial arts, and weapons of destruction, rather than negotiation and communication. Arnold Schwarzenegger, Jean Claude Van Damme, Sylvester Stallone, and Steven Seagal do not portray messages of cooperation and mediation. They illustrate conflict resolution through annihilation and victimization. I don't know if these are rationalizations or reasons. Perhaps, I'll never know! It merely confirms what we have been realizing of late, that models of male socialization need to continue to be examined and redefined.

My son's injuries have healed and my rage has faded. Zack seems to have to recovered more quickly than I have and our lives go on. He is still a gentle, happy young man. I continue to worry about him. We have been able to forgive but we will never be able to forget.

I am just so thankful that he will be able to grow up.

J. Neil Tift is the co-founder and Director of the Fathers' Resource Center in Minneapolis, Minnesota. The Center helps men find the inner resources to be the kind of father that their children need. Tift is a family mediator, has a Master of Arts Degree in Counseling Psychology and is the father of three and grandfather of three.

Reprinted with permission from Father's Resource Center, *Father Times*, Volume 2 Issue 2, Fall 1993. Copyright 1995.

Out of the Cold

The San Diego Padres were in the heat of a pennant chase and pitcher Bob Tewksbury knew every game mattered more than the previous one. What mattered more to his five-year old son, however, dwarfed the importance of throwing strikes to win a ball game.

In the months leading up to the season, "Tewks" was in the role of "Mr. Mom" for his two children. His only break occurred when his wife would take the youngsters for a couple of hours. That enabled him to run a few miles to build his stamina and leg power for spring training. He stressed how much he needed the free time, not only to exercise, but for mental relaxation.

His son was learning how to ice skate. In recent weeks, a chair had been used to help him maintain balance while learning how to glide on ice.

This particular lesson did not go well. The boy tried his best, but he kept falling. He was a picture of discouragement.

Tewks, exhausted from running six miles and tending to his three - year old daughter, sensed the ride home would be tense.

The ice-skating session reached a conclusion. He did his best to remain calm. His son was nearly in tears because of frustration.

It was only a few months ago that Tewksbury was struggling in the big leagues. He was unable to throw strikes consistently. Some kind words about hard work from a teammate supplied a boost of confidence. It helped him to get back in the proverbial groove.

"Griffin," he said to his son, *"Who scored six goals in a youth soccer game last summer?"*
The boy's eyes sparkled. *"I did."*
"And son, who is the best pitcher in the big leagues?"
"That's easy dad." the boy said. *"You are!"*
"Who can get a hit off me anytime?"
"I can!" The father and son hugged. Tears of joy replaced beads of sadness.
"Son, I know you can skate. Let's try again!"

The youngster, now somewhat relaxed, went back out to the rink. Over the next few minutes, young Griffin must have fallen a dozen times. With each slip the boy cracked a smile as his father said, *"Kerplunk."*

Moments later, the only sounds were blades cutting the ice. The boy was staying on his skates. He found his stride and kept his balance. *"Dad,"* the boy cried, *"I can skate. This is great! I can skate!"* His father smiled to himself, *"I finally know how to be a dad... and it's great!"*

John Reardon, the author of *All-Star Dads*, is an award winning elementary school principal with 35 years in education. *All-Star Dads* includes over 100 interviews with former and present major league baseball players. The book features techniques for dads to have success. Contact Reardon at (860) 583–0382 or write to him at 386 Ivy Drive, Bristol, CT. 06010

Reprinted with permission from All-Star Dads

The Effective Praise Method

1. Look at your child.

2. Move close physically.

3. Smile.

4. Say lots of nice things.

5. Praise behavior, not child.

6. Show physical affection.

7. Praise immediately.

● ● ● ● ● ● ● ● ● ● ● ● ● ● ● ●

Reprinted from Effec*tive Black Parenting, Parent's Handbook,* Dr. Kerby T. Alvy, CICC, (800) 325–CICC on the internet www.cicc.org

When kids interact with dads!

Girls who have positive paternal involvement are three times less likely to become teenage mothers.

Boys with involved dads are less likely to grow up unemployed, incarcerated or uninvolved with their own children.

Kids who team up with dads are less likely to drop out of high school. .

For more information on the project DADS call or write:

DADS DO MAKE A DIFFERENCE

99 Pratt Street #624, Hartford, CT 06103

(860) 231–2288 or fax (860) 665–0293

Web site: www.dss.state.ct.us/dadsdo

Uniting Fathers, Children, and Schools

It is time to make conscious efforts to bring fathers, children, and schools together. Studies suggest that how men relate to children is influenced by how they perceive themselves, how others perceive them, and whether or not they have a support system.

Let us start with language. We can begin to actively and positively incorporate the words;   men, fathers, dads, step-fathers, male role models, and foster fathers. There can be many types of significant father figures in the lives of children, i.e., uncle, biological father, grandfather, mom's boyfriend, or adopted dad. School text books, academic records, handouts, and parent-teacher conferences can reflect this understanding, and can send a very healthy message. Avoid saying fathers "baby-sit" their own children, they "father their own children."

We can recognize and celebrate the fact that father involvement benefits both male and female children. It also helps families, communities, and our society to turn the hearts of fathers toward the children, and the hearts of children toward the fathers.

What schools can do:

✎   Encourage fathers to visit schools by making PTA meetings especially welcoming to them.

✎   Hold meetings at times that work for fathers' schedules. Having a "dad rep" to school board meetings, or district-wide events is one way to honor the involvement of healthy fathers.

✎   Involve grandfathers and father figures in special events at school. Make time to send welcoming invites to these men. Mail invites instead of having the child bring them home.

✎   Ask all staff at the school to be observant with assigned texts, school records and handouts to insure they avoid negative stereotypes of males.

✎   Declare one day of the year to be "Fathers in Schools Day."

✎   Encourage fathers to share their arts or crafts with the school children. Find ways to weave their gifts into curriculum in affirming ways to the children and the fathers.

Invite fathers from different countries or who speak different languages to teach a brief unit on their culture and language.

Jeffry Jeanetta-Wark, MA., LICSW holds a Masters Degree in Clinical Social Work. As a practicing Psychotherapist/Social Worker, he works with families. He is a Curriculum Trainer for the Dads Make A Difference Project, and co-founder of the Young Fathers' Network.

What fathers can do with their children:

Create memory keep-sake boxes. This is excellent for children to keep letters, mementos, special photos, even video tapes of you if you live a long distance away.

Take a walk together. Keep a journal and record the sights, or sounds around you. Try to identify any noises that you may hear.

Keep a journal of books that you read together and draw your favorite parts of certain stories in the journal.

Create spiderwebs and dream catchers for the spring or fall.

Plant a tree together.

By the end of kindergarten, your six-year-old will have spent 52,000 hours outside school and 700 hours in school. You are truly your child's most important teacher!

notes

START RIGHT!

Untitled - In Honor of My Daughter 48
Sharon Loftspring

Your Unborn Baby as An Active Learner 49
Thomas Armstrong, Ph.D.

You are Your Child's First Teacher 50
Family Connections, AEL

How Your Toddler Learns 51
Thomas Armstrong, Ph.D.

Raising a Thinking Child 52
Myrna B. Shure, Ph.D.

A Healthy Start for your New Baby 55
Sally Goldberg, Ph.D.

**Eight Things You Should Expect From
Your Child Care Provider** 57

The Orange 58
Armando Sanchez

The Magic of Reading Begins Young 61

Children Learn by Playing 63
Family Connections, AEL

Tips for Choosing a Safe Toy 64
Egleston Children's Health Care System

Science and Math at Home 65
Project Prism

Little Teachable Moments 66
Ruth Bowdoin

Untitled
In Honor of My Daughter, Eland

I may be only one month old,
But I am very wise.
'Cause I have witnessed something grand
With my own two eyes.

The very day that I was born,
My Grandma came to town.
She stayed with us for one whole week
And never once sat down.

She grocery-shopped and cooked our meals.
She let my Mommy nap.
And when I fussed for hours on end,
She held me in her lap.

She played with Ethan every day.
(That's my big brother - he's two)
Then Mom and Dad could deal with me
As soon as I'd Boo Hoo
And when she left, I asked my Mom
If Grandma ever stopped.
Mom answered that a mother's love
Could never quite be topped.

I watched my Grandma care for Mom
So Mom could care for me.
And I hope someday that I'll pass on
Those loving qualities.

Sharon Loftspring

Your Unborn Baby As An Active Learner

Recent research indicates that a growing fetus is more than an unfeeling organism, but that it is actually an active learner!

Experiments done with fiber optics, for example, show that the fetus turns away when light is shined on it; other studies show an increase in heart rate and changes in the movement in the fetus when loud music is played, or when the mother is experiencing stress.

These observations suggest that even before birth there are specific behaviors being modified and changed in response to experience, and that the fetus is in the process of learning all about them.

You can take advantage of these findings and use your pregnancy as an opportunity to begin the process of educating your child.

First, sing or hum softly to your fetus; the sounds provide an introduction to rhythm and tone that will be important for later language development.

Second, avoid highly stressful situations which can expose your fetus to hormone levels that block prenatal learning.

Finally, pursue your own learning activities, whatever they are. While the fetus will not learn directly from these experiences, your own mental attitude will be a kind of comfort and security. It will provide the basis for a positive attitude toward learning after the baby is born.

Dr. Thomas Armstrong is a psychologist, learning specialist and nationally-known expert in the fields of human development and learning. His familiar books include, *In Their Own Way, The Radiant Child, 7 Kinds of Smart, The Myth of ADD Child,* and *Awakening Your Child's Natural Genius.* His columns have appeared in *Parenting Magazine, Ladies Home Journal, Family Circle* and others. For more information call (800) 753–6667 or access him on the internet at http://www.tnpc.com

---

You Are Your Child's First Teacher

You are your child's first and most important teacher. You know your children better than anyone else does and have a special interest in their welfare. You want what is best for them. You are their first role model, the first person from whom they hear language, the first to feed and dress them. They come to you for comfort when they hurt. They count on you to keep them safe and warm.

When your children start to school, they already know how to walk, how to get things they need by asking for them. They learned at home, eagerly. Children naturally love to learn, because they want to make sense of their world.

Remember when they started to walk? Those first steps were pretty wobbly, but you didn't say, "No, don't do it that way. That's wrong, or you'll fall." You smiled, and applauded, and carried on as if no child had ever before done this thing called walking nearly so well!

Children learn most and best in that kind of loving, supporting, approving environment. They learn through discovery. Playing with blocks they learn about sizes, shapes, and colors. They notice how things are related to each other. They pretend: a stick becomes a horse to be ridden; a cardboard box becomes a TV set.

Play is the very foundation for academic learning. It is children's work, their time to explore, their chance to develop muscle skills. Parents sometimes worry that their children's early school experiences don't look serious. They wonder where the workbooks are.

Researchers have found that memorization and drill, rather than being good preparation for later schooling, may cause children to miss important steps in development. So don't worry if your child's early schooling doesn't look like work. Play is children's work–some of the most important work they will ever do.

For more information about *Family Connections* early learning materials, contact the Appalachia Educational Laboratory. Call toll free at (800) 624–9120 to receive a brochure and free sample of *Family Connections*. Materials are available in English and Spanish.

How Your Toddler Learns

Every toddler is an active learner. With their new found ability to walk around, they are in a whole new relationship with the world and can explore new territory like an old world adventurer. Through their falls, their bumps, and their triumphs and discoveries, they're learning how the world works and how their own emerging self can help it work even better.

Give them lots of concrete learning materials, things they can pick up, roll, punch, stack, squeeze, bounce, pound, push, pull, and in other ways interact with. They don't need to be brightly colored fancy educational toys. Some simple household items will delight a toddler. The whole world is brand new for them.

While much of their behavior may seem haphazard to you, there's actually a lot of intelligence going on in even the simplest of acts. When your toddler picks up an object, they're forming new associations to it and creating first ideas about how the object relates to previous things they have picked up. These new discoveries become part of their inquiring mind and fuel drive toward mastery and accomplishment.

Dr. Thomas Armstrong

Raising A Thinking Child

Think of a problem you had recently with a spouse, a co-worker, a friend, your child - anyone, really. Think about how you felt before the problem was resolved–anxious, worried, angry, frustrated? Now think about how you felt after the problem was solved–relieved, happy, proud? Imagine if problem after problem remained unresolved. How might that begin to affect how you feel–and what you might do–over time? Perhaps you might feel inadequate and helpless and begin to act out in socially unacceptable ways. This is how children feel when they can't successfully resolve problems that come up with other people.

Over 20 years of research has shown that, as early as age 4, children can learn that behavior has causes, that people have feelings, and that there is more than one way to solve a problem. They can also decide whether an idea is a good one. In my book,

"Raising A Thinking Child" I show parents how they can affect their children's social adjustment by encouraging them to think. I'm talking about a very special kind of thinking, the kind involved in solving everyday problems that come up with others.

I Can Problem Solve (ICPS), designed for kindergarten-primary and intermediate elementary grades, shows teachers and parents how to help children learn to solve the problems they have with others. Its underlying goal is to help children learn how to think, not what to think. It does not tell them what to do when a conflict or other problem situation comes up. Rather, it gives children ways to talk about their view of problems and think problems through.

When children learn to use problem-solving thinking, their social adjustment improves, with significant reductions in nagging and demanding, emotional upset, and social withdrawal. Children become more able to wait, share, and take turns, as well as to get along with others. Regardless of temperament, children become better liked and more aware of, even genuinely concerned about the feelings of others.

learning ICPS Talk

Familiarize your child with the **Two-Things-at-the-Same-Time Game**. This game can be played at the dinner table, while in the car, anywhere.

First say, "I can eat my food (EAT FOOD) and look at you (LOOK AT CHILD) **at the same time.**" "I can drive the car and smile (SMILE) **at the same time.**"

Then ask your child, "What can you do **at the same time?**"

Now say, "I can **not** eat my food and drink my water **at the same time.** I can **not** drive the car and stand up **at the same time.**"

Let your child have fun making up lots of things he or she can and can not do **at the same time.**

Now, play with the word "**Different.**" This is a fork. This is a spoon. Are these the **same** thing or something **different?**" Make up examples of things that are "**different**" in any setting.

Using ICPS Talk

The next time your child interrupts while you are on the telephone, instead of telling your child you are on the phone, or suggesting watching TV (which your child will likely refuse), you can ask:

"Can I talk to you and on the phone **at the same time**?"

"Can you think of something **different** to do while you wait?"

Too often we offer an answer, instead of helping children exercise their minds. Kids can think for themselves as early as age three or four. They'll feel pride instead of anger and frustration.

Help your child avoid frustration and failure by trying out this idea the next time an argument over a toy comes up with siblings or friends.

Parent: (To Child 1) What happened? What's the matter?

Child 1: (Responds)

Parent: (To child 2) What do you think happened?

Child 2: (Responds)

Parent: Do you see this the **same** way or a **different** way?

Child 1 or 2: (Responds)

Either response **"same"** or **"different,"** can be followed with:

Parent: Oh, we have a problem. Can you think of a way to solve it? Is that a **good idea** or **not a good idea?**

Try focusing on internal versus external consequences when asking what might happen next. If the child says, "I'll get punished," ask, "What else?" Try to encourage answers like "I'll get hurt," "He'll get hurt," or "The wall will get dirty," and so on.

___

Dr. Shure, a developmental psychologist, is a professor of psychology at Allegheny University of Health Science in Philadelphia, Pennsylvania. Her acclaimed **I Can Problem Solve (ICPS)** program for parents and teachers, and her pioneering research with George Spivack have won her four national awards: one from the National Mental Health Association (1982) and three from the American Psychological Association (1984, 1986, 1994). Dr. Shure is also a media consultant on issues relating to mental health and prevention in our nation's youth. She is the author of the national best-seller, *Raising a Thinking Child,* winner of a 1996 Parents' Choice Award. To contact Dr. Shure, write to her at Allegheny University, Broad & Vine MS-626. Philadelphia, PA 19102, or call her at (215) 762-7205.

I can Problem Solve: An Interpersonal Cognitive Problem-Solving Program (Preschool, Kindergarten, Primary, and Intermediate Elementary Grades) are available from Research Press, (800) 519-2707. To order the book, *Raising a Thinking Child,* call (212) 654-8828. Also available in your local bookstores.

___

A Healthy Start For Your New Baby

Good Nutrition is key. It requires a balanced diet of natural foods. Nursing, or its substitute the bottle, is ideal through the first six months of life. At around six months of age, it is recommended to continue nursing along with the introduction little by little of solid foods. A mashed banana is an ideal first food because it is easy to digest, easy to prepare, readily available, natural, and not too expensive. After that, other fruits mashed should be introduced one at a time. Soon vegetables, also mashed, should be given. Before long, at about one year of age, your toddler can eat soft meats, many fruits and vegetables, and whole grain breads and cereals. The texture of foods should evolve gradually from soft to lumpy, to bite-size chunks, and then to traditional consistencies.

Exercise is important. If children are introduced early, starting as a baby, to exercise activities, they will learn to live their lives with exercise. In the early years our playgrounds are a child's paradise. Specialized equipment is provided to give a child the opportunity to move his body in every direction - up and down on a slide and seesaw, back and forth on a swing, around on a merry-go-round, and in every direction on a jungle-gym. A balance beam is there to develop muscles as well. We can start with small babies helping them to roll over, sit up, stand and walk. Every bouncing activity is loved and beneficial at the same time.

Adequate rest is vital. Just as it is recommended to introduce children as early as possible to positive nutrition habits and exercise routines, so it is important to work at helping them develop sleep routines from the earliest days. While these routines will change as the baby grows, the concept will remain the same. Sleep is a necessary part of human existence, important for high functioning in all areas of waking life. If you have any hesitation about this aspect of life's experiences, reflect back on how you feel after a good night's sleep, a much needed nap, or a hectic day followed by an opportunity to rest and sleep.

While these numbers may vary from individual to individual and from time to time, a rule of thumb to follow is about eight hours a night for adults, 10 for school age children, 11 for preschoolers plus a nap, 12 for toddlers plus a nap, and 13 for infants plus two naps.

Dr. Sally Goldberg teaches early childhood education in the Graduate Teacher Education Program (GTEP) at Florida's Nova Southeastern University, writes a bimonthly column for *Florida Baby* magazine and serves on the boards of directors of several major professional organizations. She is well known for **Interactive Parenting**, the cable TV series she created, produced and hosted. In her private practice, Dr. Goldberg helps parents with the education, growth and development of their children. She can be contacted at Sally R. Goldberg & Associates, Inc. 6819 SW 81st Street, Suite E, Miami, Florida 33143–7707. Telephone: (305) 663–4746. On the internet at http://www.drsally.com/

Help Keep Your Child Healthy. . . Immunize!

Immunizations (shots or medicine) are very important and are one of the best and cheapest ways to prevent diseases. Children must have immunizations to attend day care or school.

Children in the United States should get immunizations for 10 childhood diseases: diphtheria, tetanus, pertussis (DTP or DTaP), polio, Haemophilus influenzae type b (Hib), measles, mumps, rubella, hepatitis B, and varicella (chicken pox).

You can get immunizations for your child from your child's doctor or at the health department near you.

Call your health department or your child's doctor to see when your child needs to be immunized.

Eight Things You Should Expect From Your Child Care Provider

Whether your child is cared for by a baby-sitter in your home, a family day-care provider in her home, or a number of people in a child-care center, you should be able to expect certain things.

1. Open communications. Providers should give you frequent and full updates on your child's progress and problems. They should welcome your questions and ask you questions about how they can help your child.

2. Open access to their home or center. You must be welcome to drop in anytime, even without calling. Providers also should allow parents to make a reasonable number of phone calls to check on their children's well-being, in case of illness or if there's a special problem such as separation anxiety.

3. Safety for your child. Providers should take all possible precautions to keep children safe. This includes plugging light sockets, putting away knives and other sharp objects, closing off stairways and using only safe and well-maintained equipment, among other basic safety measures. It also includes always using child-safety seats and seat belts when transporting children in cars.

4. Honesty and confidence. Providers shouldn't make commitments that they can't or don't intend to keep. They shouldn't cover up problems or accidents that occur.

5. Acceptance of parents' wishes. Providers should abide by your wishes on matters such as discipline, TV watching, adult smoking and toilet training.

6. Advance notice of any changes. Since it is often very difficult to find adequate care, providers should tell you in advance if they are going to change their hours or prices or if they are going to stop or limit the time of caring for a child.

7. Assurance that everyone in contact with the child is trustworthy and properly trained and supervised. Providers must be responsible for everyone who enters, visits, and works at their home or center.

8. No surprises. This means that your family day-care provider won't suddenly tell you that since she has taken a part-time job, her teenage daughter will watch your child three afternoons a week or that your child's favorite teacher at the center just disappears without warning or comment.

The Orange

A child takes an orange from the refrigerator, peels it slightly, and begins to squeeze it. Brown juice pours out! *"The orange is spoiled!"* screams the child's parent, and grabs it from his hand.

I identify with that story. When my son, behaving like a child, did something that made me angry, impatience and anger poured out of me. I now know like the orange, the problem is inside of me.

As I peeled away the layers of my soul, the deeper issues of personal responsibility and low self esteem revealed themselves. When I accept responsibility for the way I react and for my behavior, I can prevent the *brown juice* from pouring out of me. I can be different with my son and, by example, he will be different too. My son followed my example. My anger and yelling made him feel inadequate.

Interaction with other parents in Parents Anonymous helped me to understand what I was doing and that I could control my anger. It is possible to learn new behaviors and, in turn, help our children learn them, too.

Since I cannot teach what I am not, I have become mindful of my thoughts, feelings and behavior. Both my son and I have taken our lives back.

Now I know that when I feel squeezed by my child's behavior, the juice that flows will be a bright orange!

Armando Sanchez is a Parents Anonymous parent. For information about Parents Anonymous, the nation's oldest and largest child abuse prevention organization call (909) 621–6184, or check for local chapters in your area.

Reprinted and adapted from
The Parent Networker, *Spring 1997.*
Parents Anonymous, Inc.

Family Connections NOW Available for Parents

Since 1992, preschool and kindergarten programs all over the country have been using the *Family Connections* learning guides. Families and their young children are having fun learning together with these materials. Until now, *Family Connections* was available only to educational programs. Now, these colorful, user-friendly learning guides are available in a notebook for parents.

The *Family Connections Parent Notebook* is available in three volumes. *Family Connections 1* is for families of preschool children. *Relaciones Familiares 1* is the Spanish-language version. *Family Connections 2* is for parents with kindergarten children.

Each notebook contains a set of 30 four-page learning guides, plus tips on using them. Each guide has

- a MESSAGE to parents,

- one or more READ-ALOUD selections, and

- ACTIVITIES that are fun for parent and child.

The *Family Connections* notebooks are $12.95 each ($9.95 without 3-ring binder), plus $4.00 shipping and handling. **Be sure to specify which volume(s) you desire.** Orders must be prepaid by check, money order, or credit card. Send orders to:

AEL • Family Connections
P. O. Box 1348, Charleston, WV 25325-1348

For more information, call 1(800)624-9120, e-mail santrocl@ael.org, or visit our Web site: http://www.ael.org/rel/fc.

More than 40 million Americans, cannot read or write. They find it difficult to complete a job application, understand the directions for prescription medicine or read to their children.

To fight the problem of illiteracy in our country, 7-Eleven created *People Who Read Achieve* to increase public awareness of illiteracy, and to help local groups teach people to read.

With the help of 7-Eleven's customers, employees and suppliers, over 850 organizations have received more than $2 million in grants, helping thousands learn how to read, write and speak English.

For more information about *People Who Read Achieve*, call1-800-424-7323.

The Magic of Reading Begins Young

imagination and expands their understanding of the world. It helps them develop language and listening skills and prepares them to understand the written word. When the rhythm and melody of language become a part of a child's life, learning to read will be as natural as learning to walk and talk.

At just a few months of age, an infant can look at pictures, listen to your voice, and point to objects on cardboard pages. Guide your child by pointing to the pictures, and say the names of the various objects. By drawing attention to pictures and associating the words with both pictures and the real-world objects, your child will learn the importance of language.

Children learn to love the sound of language before they even notice the existence of printed words on a page. Reading books aloud to children stimulates their

Reading aloud is important. One expert in education has said that if parents of preschoolers read aloud to their children just 15 minutes a day it would revolutionize the schools. The Commission on Reading said that the single most important activity to create success in reading is reading aloud to children.

When should you start reading to children? It's never too early, and NOW is a good time. Young children enjoy sitting on your lap when you read to them. It's also good practice to have them sit on your left side while you point to the words. This helps them learn that we read from left to right. The single most important thing about reading is that it be a social event. Encourage questions and talk about what you are reading. Make it a time you and your child look forward to having together.

What should you read? Your child's teacher can offer suggestions. The librarian at your public library knows which books interest children at various ages. Let your child help choose books. Read books that appeal to you, too. Children like to have books read over and over again, so it helps to have books that hold your interest. Pay attention to illustrations when you choose books to read aloud. Beautiful pictures add meaning to the best books.

Finally, let your child see you reading. Modeling is a powerful teacher. If your child sees you and other adults reading for pleasure as well as to gain information, reading becomes valuable to them.

These are books that children's librarians suggest for reading aloud to preschool children. This list is courtesy of Family Connections, Appalachia Educational Laboratory. There are many other excellent books for little ones. Ask your local librarian to recommend others if these are not available at your library.

Pigs Say Oink, M. Alexander

My Five Senses, Aliki

The Bears' Vacation, Stan Berenstain

Messy, B. Bottner

The Little House, V. Burton

Olive and the Magic Hat, E. Christelow

Cars and How They Go, J. Cole

Go, Dog, Go, P.D. Eastman

What Am I?, M. Hillert

Bread and Jam for Frances, L. Hoban

Ben's Trumpet, R. Isadora

Prehistoric Pinkerton, S. Kellogg

Socks for Supper, J. Kent

A Color of His Own, Leo Lionni

Blueberries for Sal, R. McCloskey

The Quiet Farmer, M. McGee

Little Bear, E. H. Minarik

By Day and By Night, K. Pandell

Mr. and Mrs. Pig's Evening Out, M. Rayner

Sam Who Never Forgets, E. Rice

Curious George, H. A. Rey

Birthday Presents, C. Rylant

Where the Wild Things Are, Maurice Sendak (for ages 5 and 6)

Green Eggs and Ham, Dr. Seuss

I Can Read with My Eyes Shut!, Dr. Seuss

Oh, the Places You'll Go!, Dr. Seuss (for ages 5 and 6)

Sheep in a Jeep, N. Shaw

Thump and Plunk, J. Udry

Children Learn by Playing

well. It is just fun. Until they are seven or eight years old, children are more interested in what they are doing than how it turns out. They play at something until they become skilled. Then they make the activity more challenging. That way, they get to experience success and build their feelings of competence.

Young Children do not separate play, learning, and work. When young children are playing, they are learning. And they are enjoying every minute of it.

Young children's play is spontaneous. They are so eager to learn, it seems that their curiosity can't be satisfied. All too soon that curiosity and spontaneity seem to disappear. Children don't seem so eager and enthusiastic about school. We begin to hear questions about how to motivate them to learn.

How does this very sad thing happen? We make such comments as: "Quit playing around and get to work." "You can't play until you finish your work." With these comments, we teach children that learning isn't enjoyable.

From a child's point of view, play is something you don't have to do

Adults are likely to see play as a means to an end. We insist that children do a thing the correct way before they have time to explore and enjoy the means. For example, we give children coloring books and teach them to stay in the lines. Better to give them paper and crayons and let them discover the possibilities.

When you do activities, encourage imagination and creativity. Don't insist on pursuing something that isn't fun for your child. Children naturally love learning. They will continue to love it if we don't teach them that work and learning are not meant to be enjoyed.

Family Connections, Appalachia Educational Laboratory

Tips for Choosing A Safe Toy

Playtime is important for your child's healthy growth and development. To make sure your child's play time is safe and happy, please follow these guidelines when selecting a toy.

Look for toys that are right for your child's age and that encourage:

- Active play, like push or pull toys or a ball and bat.

- Hand movement play, like clay, puzzles, tea sets or action figures.

- Creative play, like paints, crayons or musical instruments.

- Learning play, like games or books.

Be aware that some toys can be dangerous for your child.

For a child who is 8 or under, avoid...

- Electrical toys with hot surfaces (toy oven sets or woodburners).

- Toys or art sets with toxic substances (oil paints, chemistry sets).

For a child who is 3 or younger, avoid...

- Small toys or toys with small removable parts that can be lodged in a child's throat.

- Toys with loose breakable parts that come off (action figures with removable parts, cars with small wheels) latex balloons (a leading cause of choking).

For an infant, avoid...

- Hanging crib and playpen toys with strings longer than 12 inches, which can strangle a child (mobiles).

- Squeeze toys, rattles and teethers small enough to become lodged in a child's throat.

- Toys not approved for infants (mini rattles used for gift wrapping).

This information was provided by the child safety experts of the Egleston Children's Health Care System, Atlanta, Georgia. For additional information about safety and products contact the U.S. Consumer Product Safety Commission, Washington, D.C. 20207 for free brochures.

Science and Math at Home

Did you know that the kinds of games you play with your preschoolers can influence whether they want to learn math and science? So can the questions you ask and the toys you give them to play with.

Bigger, smaller, higher, lower, farther, faster, slower, bouncier.

These are the words of math and science for the young child. And these are the beginnings of math and science learning.

Children are never too young to become interested in math and science. In fact, young children are natural scientists and mathematicians. They are curious. They ask questions all the time. They like to explore and experiment. When you encourage their questions and help them explore and find out the answers, you're building their interest in math and science. And children who have such experiences when they are very young develop an enjoyment and a confidence in math and science that pays off when they're older.

Here are some simple things you can do to develop a preschooler's interest in science and math.

Go for a walk with your child. Take time to notice what's around your plants, animals, ants, mosquitoes, dandelions, etc. Stop and watch. Talk about what you see.

Plant a garden with your child. Planting a garden, any size garden, is a great family activity. A garden can be a patch of dirt in the yard or a container on a window sill. Measure the space or container. Figure out where the plants will get sunlight. Count the seeds. Measure the rows. Watch the plants grow. Pick vegetables. Look for insects. Learn what plants need to be healthy. What a lot of math and science there is in gardening!

Listen to children and ask them questions about what they're seeing and doing. Children need to have time every day to tell another person about what they have seen or what they think. When your child tells you what she saw on a walk, or what he liked best about the trip to the zoo, they learn that their ideas are important to you.

Project PRISM is a program of National Urban League, Inc. in association with the National Council of La Raza, The NETWORK, Inc., and Thirteen/WNET funded by Annenberg/CPB Math and Science Project.

Little Teachable Moments

Shopping, preparing meals, doing household chores and working around the yard are all wonderful opportunities to teach your child. Here are a few "little teachable moments."

Shopping in the Grocery

Here is a wonderful laboratory for learning! It is   perfect for developing vocabulary. Fruits, vegetables, meats, bakery products, cans, cartons, boxes, and a large assortment of objects are available   as teaching tools.

You will find opportunities galore! Identifying objects, colors, sizes and a host of other things! More difficult concepts such as large-small, low-high, bottom-middle-top, back-front can be developed when your preschooler is ready.

You may find it necessary to say "No, sorry. We can't buy that. It is not on our list." You may need to endure a little cry or a big one! Even a tantrum. But, don't let embarrassment keep you from being consistent - kind, gentle but firm!   These are wonderful "teachable moments."

Walking in the Neighborhood

Young children need to become familiar with their environment. They are naturally curious. They look and see, do and touch. A flower in the yard, a blade of grass, a grain of sand or a pebble can be as fascinating as an expensive toy.

Your neighborhood may be in the country with pastures, trees, fences, and animals. Or, it could be in a town where riding around the block in a wagon is a toddler's delight. The city or housing development has traffic lights, shiny cars, and tall buildings. There is always opportunity for developing curiosity and stimulating imagination! Productive "teachable moments" are everywhere!

Helping in the Yard

While you are at work in the yard, conversations can be very productive. Leaves are falling! "Let's find the yellow ones and make a pile, the brown ones here, the green ones here!" This will keep your preschooler busy as you work and carry on conversations.

After a short while, stop and sit. Gather a group of leaves for your teaching. "See if you can find another leaf just like this one."

Show me the largest one in this group of three. Which is the smallest? Now here is a group of three. Show me the one that is different, not like the other two." (Always with approval for high responses.) Teaching likeness and differences will be helpful for developing the child's visual discrimination necessary for beginning reading.

What fun your child can have playing in a pile of fresh fallen leaves! Perhaps a toy rake would be a good tool to purchase. Helping dad or mom gives a child good feelings that can last a lifetime.

Preparing a Meal

Vocabulary building opportunities abound in the kitchen! A wise parent engages in meaningful conversation during the preparation and feeding time. No matter the stage of development–baby, toddler, preschooler or kindergartner–a nice little talk can go well with your work. It takes no more time.

Explain what you are doing and when appropriate, ask questions and encourage responses. For example, at preschool stage, your conversation could be something like this: "I am spreading this brown, delicious peanut butter on this graham cracker, very smoothly, very carefully from corner to corner. One, two, three, four, corners. Why, it's a square! See. Would you like a top on it?

Talking at Mealtime

Around the table. A family-friendly place to be! A thing of the past? It doesn't need to be! You may not feel that you have the time, but what valuable experiences you are missing! Take the time; make the time! It is well worth your effort.

Preparing, serving and sitting down with your family is a tradition too valuable to miss! Of course, it takes planning. Setting a definite time, establishing rules, teaching manners, requiring certain behaviors and remaining consistent–all are opportunities for good teaching! Even with a one parent–one child family, this experience provides for many beautiful "teachable moments!" With larger families there can be more taking turns, more listening. No eat-and-run allowed! These days will be precious memories for a lifetime and your children will be talking about it decades later!

For 30 years, Mrs. Bowdoin has been a professional educator with the Murfreesboro City Schools, Tennessee. She served as a teacher, then a supervisor of teachers and later as director of the world-renowned Classroom on Wheels. She developed the Bowdoin Method of Parent Training, which is published and distributed by Webster's International. It is used throughout the United States and in 14 countries. You can order Mrs. Bowdoin's book, *The Magical Years* for $9.95 plus S&H, call (800) 727–6833.

---

notes

notes

READY TO LEARN

Ready For School 72
Sally Goldberg, Ph.D.

What to Ask When Your Child Begins School 73
Texas PTA & Texas Education Agency

Building "Megaskills" For Success 75
Dorothy Rich, Ed.D

Kids And Money 76
Blaine Harris

Distinguished Performance Award 79
Frances Grimes Yeargin

The Magic Of Reading Aloud 80
Patricia Penn

Every Room is a Learning Place 81
Dorothy Rich, Ed.D.

Planting the Seed of Science Curiosity 83
Diane Wehrell, Ph.D.

Learning Science and Math in Your Community 85
Project PRISM

Section 4

A Word to Parents 87
Vivian Herrikan

Tell A Story! - Tips for Storytelling 88
Gladys Wright

The Piano Recital 90
Barbara Pearson

What You Should Know About Music 92
Barbara Wyatt

Taking Charge of Your T.V. 95
Critical Viewing Project

Surf Safety on the Internet 99
H. Mike Rice

The Kite 103
Andy Vu

Ready For School

It is no accident when you find a child ready for school. While children develop at different rates, there are clear markers that signal when a child is ready for school. An excellent early environment has clearly been a part of that child's life. A broad overall set of experiences is certain to have taken place. According to Dr. Sally Golderg, in her book, *"Parent Involvement Begins at Birth,"* children able to perform these tasks are ready for school.

- Know their first and last names.
- Tell their address or telephone number.
- Know their parents' or guardians' name.
- Catch a large ball most of the time.
- Run and stop on signal.
- Hop on one foot and skip.
- Hold a pencil.
- Use scissors.
- Like to write and draw (can usually write their name).
- Count (often "skip" counting by twos, fives, or ten).
- Like to tell riddles and jokes.
- Copy shapes (circles, squares, triangles, and rectangles).
- Sort things in categories by color, shape, and kind.
- Fill in the missing part (on pictures of people, figures, animals, or a house).

What to Ask When Your Child Begins School

It is helpful to know these important facts about the school and your child's classroom:

1. Ask for a handbook and information on school procedures such as:

   - Time the school day begins and ends.

   - The earliest time children may arrive at school.

   - Notifications about absences by school and by parent.

   - Permission for riding a bike to school.

   - Availability of after-school activities.

   - Yearly schedule (year-round school or traditional schedule).

   - School policies regarding such activities as visiting the classroom, disaster preparedness plan, discipline, and grading.

2. Contact your child's teacher to introduce yourself, supply needed information about your family and set up a way to communicate on a regular basis.

3. Make an appointment to ask the teacher about:

   - The amount of homework to be expected.

   - Being kept informed about your child's progress.

   - What you can do to assist your child's progress.

   - How and when to contact the teacher by phone.

   - Notification of tests and how results are used.

   - What is expected to learn academically during the school year.

   - How you can be of help to the teacher.

4. Sign up to support the school by volunteering as time allows.

5. Ask for information on the school's site-based decision-making committee/team, including who serves on the team, when it meets and how parents are able to participate or have issues placed on its agenda.

Courtesy of The Texas PTA & The Texas Education Agency

We design bridges to take people across rivers, mountains and from one place to the other. In life one can acquire an education by reading and comprehending. An education will create knowledge along with integrity, to design bridges for life which will allow you to become an engineer, architect, doctor or whatever your heart desires.

BUILDING MEGASKILLS® FOR SUCCESS

Children need to learn important basics at home to learn and keep on learning basic skills at school. Dr. Dorothy Rich calls them "MegaSkills." These are attitudes and abilities that are bigger than ordinary skills. She says; "a MegaSkill is a long-lasting achievement-enhancing skill. They help us use the other skills we learn. They act as catalysts in learning and play a strong role in determining success in school and beyond. They are the values that undergird our work ethic, our national character and our personal behavior."

She lists the following MegaSkills[1]:

CONFIDENCE:	feeling able to do it
MOTIVATION:	wanting to do it
EFFORT:	being willing to work hard
RESPONSIBILITY:	doing what's right
INITIATIVE:	moving into action
PERSEVERANCE:	completing what you start
CARING:	showing concern for others
TEAM WORK:	working with others
COMMON SENSE:	using good judgment
PROBLEM SOLVING:	putting what you know and what you can do into action

Each and every day we need to remember how much our children need us. It is so easy to forget that lifelong learning patterns are set into place during a child's early years. Let's start today to plan our children's experiences so they will, over a period of years, develop these personal traits which will cause them to be competent, successful adults.

[1]Building Children's Achievement for the Information Age, Houghton Mifflin, 1998

Kids and Money

In our society we are being bombarded with 1,001 ways to spend money on a daily basis. We buy immediately, without control as yet one more way of receiving instant gratification. "I see it, I want it, I buy it" - regardless of

. . . it has become not just important, but essential that we arm our kids with knowledge and practical application pertaining to money.

whether we have the money and with no thought for the consequence of tomorrow. With billions of marketing dollars being spent each year to persuade us and our children to buy, it has become not just important, but essential that we arm our kids with knowledge and practical application pertaining to money. We must prepare them for the subtle yet powerful influence that will hit them

regarding what to do with the money they will earn and receive throughout their lifetime.

Needs versus Wants

Teaching children to distinguish between needs and wants is becoming increasingly difficult. The media influence is so far reaching that almost everything is projected to be a need. Where young children are involved, simple games can be played with them to help them learn the difference between needs and wants. Set up small objects that represent things such as food, toys, shelter, transportation, candy. Let them distinguish between those that represent a need versus a want. As you help them begin a savings program, direct them in separating the money they will use for needs and that which can be used for wants. Help them see the choices that you as a parent have made to illustrate needs for the family versus personal wants.

Example: Even though our family loves water sports and we really want to buy a jet ski, we have other things that are more important to our family such as buying school clothes, food and paying for the house we live in. In order to get some of the extra things we want, we must all save together and then buy it when we have enough saved.

As children become older they generally recognize the difference between needs and wants but they very often have bought into the notion "I can have it all now." Advertising for electronics equipment, catalog games and toys, clothing and even music promotes "buy it today and enjoy it now, but don't worry about paying until sometime in the future." Consequently, older children often don't feel they have to make choices between needs and wants because they believe they can have it all right now. Our challenge as parents is to help them understand the steep price they are paying for buying on time, not to mention the emotional burden and poor habits that accompany such behavior.

Children of all ages need to understand, if they do not have the money available in their piggy bank, dresser drawer or bank account, they do not have the money to purchase the item they

are wanting. Going into debt for any want and even many needs is unnecessary and should not happen. Teaching children how to control impulse buying and how to evaluate the value of a purchase prior to making it is invaluable behavior that will serve them well throughout their lives and literally by putting dollars in their pocket.

Allowance and Earning

There are many ideas on how or if children should be given allowances. Each family needs to decide what works for them, however, there are three things that are important to note in making the decisions and rules that surround the subject:

1. It is important for children to be able to earn or receive their own money in some way in order for them to learn the basic principles of money management. Money is so fundamental in our society that it's critical that children have an opportunity to learn about and make decisions with money that is their own. There is a difference between money that a parent gives a child when it is asked for versus money a child has received or earned prior to the time when the child needs the money for some purpose.

2. If allowance is given, it should not be tied to routine

chores or duties around the home (i.e., making the bed, taking out the garbage, hanging up clothes ...). Children need to learn that there are certain things we each do just to make a household work, things we do just for the privilege of being part of the family, which has no monetary reward tied to it.

3.   Guidelines should be outlined, defining how all money earned or received is to be managed. Children not only need rules and guidelines, but they generally learn and progress at a more rapid pace where expectations and directions are clearly defined. The principle "give some, save some, invest some and spend some" may be a very simple starting point, directing them on what to do with the money they have which can be detailed out with specific percentage amounts as they are old enough to understand.

As parents, we can provide special projects or opportunities for children to earn money. Going to school and obtaining the very best possible education can even be used as an incentive to earn money. In a sense, school for children is like work for adults and thus, a monetary reward for outstanding work can be easily applied.

Example: A-$10.00 B-$5.00 C-0.00 below that, the child pays. Obtaining a good education is one of the most important things our children can do for themselves, helping them treat school like a job where they are responsible and get rewarded accordingly may provide an additional incentive to do so.

Managing, Saving and Setting Limits

As children have money of their own to manage, it is important for them to track how much they earn, how much they spend and how much they have remaining. They can do this in a journal or even in a check register where they write down all of the cash they spend and checks they write if they have a checking account. Tracking their financial activity, even at a young age, creates greater awareness about their financial choices and can motivate them toward saving more as they see their balance growing.

Blaine Harris is the founder, CEO and Chairman of the Board of Chequemate, International. He has been happily married for 34 years to his companion and high school sweetheart. They have three sons and one daughter, all actively involved in the Chequemate System. You may contact Mr. Harris at (800) CHK–MATE.

Distinguished Performance Award

Nowadays some children are paid cash for making good grades. My brothers and I grew up during the Depression. Money was scarce. Our mother's chief way to inspire us to higher achievement was a very special kiss on the cheek.

Whenever one of us brought home an *"A"* on a report card, an *"excellent"* written across a term paper or some other triumph, mother would say with great ceremony, *"that deserves a kiss on the cheek."* She would hold us at arm's length, admire us briefly, and then draw us close and deliver the *"smack of love."* If the accomplishment was really exceptional, she said, *"why, that's good, I think it deserves a kiss on both cheeks!"*

Then she delivered the Distinguished Performance Award most treasured in our family. A kiss on the cheek sounds simple, but it was mother's way of showing approval. Everyone likes appreciation for work well done.

Mother's award must have been successful. The four of us children accrued a total of six college degrees. All of us married. None of us divorced. We presented mother with 17 grandchildren.

Frances Grimes Yeargin
Houston, Texas

The Magic of Reading Aloud

Of all the things parents can do to help their children succeed in school, reading aloud to them is probably the most important. It makes a big difference if they see you reading, too. Start early; even very young babies enjoy having you read to them. And don't stop when they learn to read for themselves. Reading aloud is a good lifelong practice.

Read all kinds of things; books, of course, but also magazines, newspaper comics, the backs of cereal boxes. Let your children help you make shopping lists, so they see that written language is part of everyday life.

Choose books together at the library. Most libraries now will issue cards to young children. Having their own cards makes trips to the library a special treat.

When you read aloud, vary your voice. Make it high sometimes, low others. Allow time for questions and comments. Do not hurry. Be sure your child can see the pictures. Ask "what do you think will happen next?" Make reading interactive.

Every time you read aloud, you help your child improve memory skills and add vocabulary. You also send a message about how important the printed word is in all our lives.

Adapted from Family Connections by Patricia Penn, author. For information about *Family Connections* early learning materials, contact the Appalachia Educational Laboratory, (800) 624-9120

Every Room Is A Learning Place!

Every room in the home is a learning place. Here are some activities that are designed to help children develop the values, attitudes, and behaviors that determine achievement in school and beyond. They focus on the use of three particular rooms in the home - the kitchen, the bathroom, and the living room.

KITCHEN. Every kitchen–with its sink, stove, refrigerator, dishes, pots, cans and boxes–has the necessary ingredients to become a miracle place for learning. This is learning that extends from, builds on, reinforces, but does not duplicate the school.

Hidden Letters. All around the kitchen, from the cupboard to the refrigerator, from the stove to the sink, there are letters: A's, B's, F's, P's, etc. On the soup cans, on the cat food, on the cereal box, even on the soap–there are letters. Make a game of finding these letters; ask children (without tearing up the place of course) to find five A's or three C's or any number of letters. Start easy and build to harder and harder letter combinations to find.

Cooking Up Directions. You don't just cook a "dish" you have to read directions to know what comes first, second and so on. Select a simple recipe with your child, perhaps Jell-O, instant pudding, or canned soup. Follow the directions step by step - reading them aloud as you go along.

BATHROOM. Label, label. Reading is all around–on medicine and cleanser labels. These are the very words that children have to be taught to read carefully. Spend time with the children, as they take their baths or brush their teeth, to read these labels carefully. These can be a matter of life and death.

Float and Sink. Which object when plopped into the water will float? Which object will sink? Try different soaps, a dry sock, a full plastic bottle of shampoo, a wet sponge, a dry sponge, an empty bottle. The important part of this game is to have children think (guess) beforehand which objects will float or sink and then test out this hypothesis–true scientific method!

Weigh Me. Have children make some guesses first about how heavy they think different things weigh - including their own body and parents' bodies, too. Weigh the wastebasket, weigh clothing just taken off, weigh a full glass of water.

Matching and piling. Laundry contains mathematics: match the socks, count them; count the sheets and fold them into fractional pares, down to half down to one-quarter. PS: The laundry gets put away at the same time.

LIVING\FAMILY ROOM.

Phonics Bingo Games: Put beginning consonants on shirt cardboard, start with the easier ones: B, P, S, R. Call out the sounds for BINGO - use words, B - bat, R - rat. Ask players to cover the letters called. Make the games more complex as children gain greater skill.

Cartoons Cut-Ups. Cut up comic squares and ask children to rearrange them in logical or illogical sequence. Cut out the words the characters speak and have children fill in their own words. This is good fun and good writing practice.

Measure for Pleasure. The world is filled with things and space to measure: how tall is the lamp? how wide is the room? Use yardsticks, tape measure. Jot down the results to share with the family.

Catalog Shopping Spree. Let's say you have 25 dollars (hypothetical) to spend. Look through a new or old mail order catalog and select your purchases; add them up; what have you left? Have you overspent? How do other members of the family decide to spend their money. Compare and contrast purchases.

TV and the World. Tie current events and map use with TV watching. Post a world map next to the TV set, so children can immediately look up references to world news spots. Keep reference books close by, too. These offer tidbits of knowledge, when children's curiosity is high.

Dorothy Rich, Ed.D., called the "Dr. Spock of Education," is founder and president of the nonprofit Home and School Institute (HSI) based in Washington, D.C. Recognized internationally for her expertise in family education involvement, she is the author of the original MegaSkills and the developer of the MegaSkills training programs. The focus of her work is on helping families and educators team together to build achievement for children and adults. For additional information, you may contact Dr. Rich at The MegaSkills Education Center, Home and School Institute, 1500 Massachusetts Avenue, NW, Washington, DC 20005 (202) 466-3633. On the internet at http://www.MegaSkillsHSI.org

---

Planting the Seed of Science Curiosity

Parents can help to strengthen their child's understanding of scientific concepts in and around the home. Children are naturally curious about science and the world around them. It doesn't matter whether they are in preschool or high school, they continue to ask questions about their environment. Parents are bombarded on a daily basis with a myriad of questions from their children. From the most simple question to the most abstract parents can be assured that their child will have a daily science question for them to ponder over. You can help to nurture your child's natural curiosity towards science no matter heir age by providing a conducive environment in and around the home for learning scientific concepts.

As a parent, we play a vital role in how much science our child will be exposed to on a daily basis. Look around your home, backyard, or balcony. Does your home have the essential tools to nurture that curious scientist? Is there a microscope around the house for exploring such simple objects as a piece of salt, water sample, or a bird feather? Have you encouraged your child to start a collection of objects found in nature such as, rocks, feathers, exoskeletons , and fossils.

Build or purchase some simple storage boxes for your child's nature collections. Empty film canisters, jewelry containers, and egg cartons make fantastic storage containers and what's better they're free and you're also recycling.

Check out the contents of your kitchen cupboards for possible ingredients for chemical and physical science investigations. Believe it or not, some of the most exciting experiments can be undertaken right in your kitchen with such simple household ingredients as baking soda, corn starch, vinegar, water, and salt. Next time you're cleaning out the garage or "junk drawers" in your home, store aside items such as wire, batteries, light bulbs, plastic containers, and rubberbands. All of these items can be used for exploring a wide array of scientific concepts.

Take an exploratory hike in your backyard or local park. Does your yard look appealing to wildlife of all types? Butterflies, birds, and squirrels are just a few of the many living creatures that will visit your backyard if you've gone the few extra steps to make it inviting by planting trees and flowers that attract a variety of wildlife. Do you have a water source for birds to bathe in? How about bird and squirrel feeders ? If not, birdbaths and feeders are fun and easy to construct with your child.

The long-term benefits of engaging in hands-on science with your child at home are many. Both parent and child gain additional scientific knowledge and create stronger bonds.

The author, Dr. Diana Wehrell has a Ph.D. in Science Education and is a self-employed science education consultant who travels throughout the state of Florida and the United States providing hands-on science programs and family science workshops for teachers, parents, and students of all ages.

For further information about family science programs contact Dr. Diana Wehrell at Mobile Science Education Consulting Services, 200 N. First Street, Cocoa Beach, Florida 32931, Phone and Fax: (407) 799-9004, e-mail address: mobilescience@iu.net

Special Opportunity for Schools

In May 1997, the Federal Communications Commission (FCC) approved a rule (known as the E-rate) giving schools 20 to 90 percent discounts in access charges to the Internet and telecommunications services, including wiring school buildings for the Internet. (The amount of the discount depends on how many low-income students a school serves and whether it is located in a rural, suburban, or urban area). Starting in January 1998, more than $2 billion a year will be available for the discounts (see http://www.fcc.gov/learnnet/ and http://www.ed.gov/Technology/ for more information).

To apply for a discount, a school must have a technology plan that explains how the school will integrate technology into the curriculum. The plan must also address hardware, software, training, and maintenance issues. As a parent, you can play an active role in helping your school develop a technology plan.

Learning Science and Math in Your Community

Think of your neighborhood as a science and math resource. A tour of the factory or shop where a family member works, an insect hunt in the playground, park, or lot are examples of places to learn science. Think of the "hands-on" math problems you can make up at a busy intersection. How many vehicles go through the intersection each time the light is green? How long is the light green? Predict the number of vehicles that will go through that intersection in fifteen minutes or half an hour. Once you begin looking for ways to use your neighborhood as a place to learn science and math, you will discover more and more! Find local businesses where students can get behind the scenes.

Students can talk with people who work there, and discover the uses of science and math. For example, the dry cleaner uses chemicals. What happens to the used chemicals? How do chemicals remove stains? The grocer sells food. How are fruits, vegetables, and meat kept fresh? Is there some kind of inspection process? What happens to food after the expiration date? How much of the price of each item is profit? What expenses are there for the grocery store owner?

Use buildings in your community to teach science and math concepts. Discover what materials the buildings in your community are made of. Wood? Concrete? Adobe? Brick? Granite? Sandstone? Steel?

Glass? Explore reasons for using these materials. Buildings can create lots of math activities. A young child can copy a building using blocks. Older students can estimate, count, and measure windows, doors, stairs, floors, and the many other features of buildings. Buildings provide homes for animals besides people! Go on a hunt for insects, birds, or other animals that live in and around buildings in your community. You'll be surprised at how many you can find!

Discover what happens to waste and trash in your community. Where does the sewage go when it leaves your home? Does your community have a recycling program? What materials are collected for recycling? Why aren't more things recycled? See if there is a landfill you could arrange to take a group of children to visit. Perhaps your family can start a recycling project at home or in the neighborhood.

Find out where drinking water comes from in your community and how it is kept safe to drink. Contact your local department of public works or the town or city hall for help getting this information. Once you find out where the water comes from, get out a map and locate the reservoir, river, or water treatment plant. Find out if there is a water treatment facility you could visit. Does the water in the fire hydrants come from the same place? How does a hydrant work?

Make and use maps

Making a map of a room in your home involves measuring and geometry. When you choose shapes to represent furniture, windows, or doors, you are using symbols. These are important mathematical ideas. Making a map of the neighborhood can be a good family project. At the same time you use math, you can learn more about what is in your neighborhood.

Project PRISM is a program of National Urban League, Inc. in association with the National Council of La Raza, The NETWORK, Inc., and Thirteen/WNET funded by Annenberg/CPB Math and Science Project.

A Word to Parents

"I got two A's," the small boy cried.
His voice was filled with glee.
His father very bluntly asked,
"Why didn't you get three?"
"Mom, I've got the dishes done!"
The girl called from the door.
Her mother very calmly said,
"And did you sweep the floor?"
I've mowed the grass," the tall boy said,
"And put the mower away!"
His mother asked him with a shrug,
"Did you clean off the clay?"
The children in the house next door
seem happy and content.
The same things happened over there,
but this is how it went.
"I got two A's," the small boy cried.
His voice was filled with glee.
His father proudly said, "That's great!
I'm glad you live with me!"
"Mom, I've got the dishes done!"
The girl called from the door.
Her mother smiled and softly said,
"Each day I love you more."
"I've mowed the grass," the tall boy said.
"And put the mower away!"
His mother answered with much joy.
"You've made me happy today!"
Children desire a little praise.
For tasks they're asked to do.
If they're to lead a happy life,
So much depends on you.

Vivian Herrikan

Tell a Story!

Children love stories, whether they are in books or in a movie or the kind grandparents tell. Storytelling is an oral tradition. It passes on values, traditions, develops literary skills, records history, stretches the imagination and bonds. There are many spaces where storytelling can fit into our lives. Try using storytelling during long drives, while waiting at the airport, or at bedtime.

Here are some tips

- Share your pride in your family's culture and tradition with your children.

- Talk about what you read. It is another way to help your child develop language and listening skills.

- Select a special storybook. Ask your children to help you. Link stories to the past and the world today.

- Teach your children your favorite childhood stories.

- Look at picture books together, make up stories as you go along.

- Gather old family photos. Make a collage out of pictures; select things that matter to you and your family.

- Write down family stories, tape family members, interview them. Have your child ask questions.

Parenting is not an instant; it is something we learn everyday. Teach your children what you already know. . . When parents teach, children learn. Pass it on! Tell your child a story today.

Here are some tips for successful storytelling from *"The Parent's Guide to Storytelling"* (HarperCollins Publishers) by Margaret Read MacDonald.

Tell the story in your own words. Don't worry about getting the story "right." There is no right way to tell a story. Folktales have been passed from person to person for thousands of years. Every single teller changes the story to fit. Just tell the story in your own way.

Eye contact. When telling stories to a group of children, it helps to make good eye contact with the audience as you tell. But when telling to one or two children, it may be more comfortable to hold them on your lap or by your side. Let your words alone reach them as you all look inward to the story.

Bounces and finger plays. When telling to very small children, you may want to incorporate bounces or other tactile elements into your story. "The Gingerbread Man," for example could be told while you hold the child on your lap, bouncing the child when the Gingerbread Man chants and runs.

Begin story play with babies and toddlers through use of simple finger play stories. These involve manipulation of the child's hand during the telling.

Audience participation: If stories have repetitive elements, children may enjoy chiming in on the refrains. Pause, and with a glance, encourage your listeners to join you.

When the children are full of energy, audience participation works well. At times your listeners may even want to act out the parts while you tell the story. However, when these same stories are used at bedtime, a quieter telling, without the participation may be more effective.

Remember, the heart of the story is what counts. If you are willing to take the time to share a story, your child will want to listen.

Gladys Wright teaches parenting skills and is a site coordinator for the Family Resource Center at Chase School in Waterbury, Connecticut. (203) 573-6646

GEORGIA BABIES WELCOMED ON A GOOD NOTE

"There is research that links the study of music to better school performance and higher scores on college entrance exams. There's even a study called the "Mozart effect" that showed after college students listened to Mozart piano sonata for 10 minutes, their IQ score increased by nine points. Some argue that it didn't last, but no one doubts that listening to music, especially at a very early age, affects the spatial-temporal reasoning that underlies math, engineering and chess.

So I propose that the parents of every baby born in Georgia –over 100,000 a year –be given a cassette or CD of music to be played often in the baby's presence. It's not a big ticket item in the budget–only $105,000–but I believe it can help Georgia children to excel."

Governor Zell Miller
FY 99 Budget Address
January 13, 1998

The Piano Recital

education was to continue for another eight years, but the real lesson I learned from this experience had nothing to do with music.

I had been taking piano lessons for only six weeks when the annual recital was to be presented. Since I was the youngest participant and had been taking lessons for the shortest length of time, I was to be the last performer on the program. My selection was titled "Flow Gently, Sweet Afton," the last song in my first book of one-handed melodies.

In the spring of 1954, I felt the world would be complete if only I could be allowed to take piano lessons. My parents gave in to my dogged persistence, even though the money for those lessons should have gone for any number of real necessities. My musical

Anyone who grows up on a farm in southern Illinois knows where a farmer will be on a hot, sunny afternoon in June. The wheat must be harvested when it is ready and the weather is right. There is no putting it off for anything, least of all a piano recital for a five-year-old girl who has been taking lessons for a little more than a month. No one had to tell me that the only member of my family in attendance would be my mother. That's just the way it was. In fact, there would be no fathers in attendance. Each would be in his own field on a combine, or working with a neighbor to bring in the crop.

It has been over forty years since that hot, Sunday afternoon, but I can still see the new pink skirt my mother had so lovingly sewn for me to wear and the excitement of all of us who were to perform. I remember the nervous giggles as we peeked through the door into the audience seated on folding chairs in the classroom on the third floor of a stifling hot grade school. Most of all, I remember the surprise and wonder I felt as I gazed upon the loving face of my very proud father seated in the front row. It did not matter at all to him that he was the only man in the room.

Yes, there he was. I could see by the look on his face, that there was no place he'd rather be. This hard working farmer who should have been on his tractor was sitting down on a wooden chair in a suit and tie, with sweat running down his face as he waited for the very last piano student of Sister Mary Louise to play her song that would last all of sixteen seconds.

As soon as we returned home, my father changed his clothes and headed for the wheat field, where every other father had been that afternoon. He had lost probably three precious hours of work in the field, but the lesson he taught me that day was worth more than any wheat he may have harvested in those three hours.

Without saying a word, my father taught me that a parent's "presence" is worth more than any "presents" ever given. Now that I have children of my own, I remember that recital Sunday every time I feel that I'm "too tired," "too busy" or "too stressed" to go to one more Cub Scout meeting, talent show, open house, or cheerleading practice. The image of that dear, sweet man waiting so patiently for me to play my precious song urges me to put on my coat and just go. Nothing is as important to a child as having parents present to witness even the smallest of accomplishments. If God would allow me to relive just one childhood memory, I would have no trouble making my choice.

Barbara Pearson
St. John, IN

What You Should Know About Music and Your Child

Music is powerful. It influences the conscious and the subconscious. Think how you feel when you hear the drum beat in martial music or the soft tomes in a lullaby. A lullaby comforts children and lulls them to sleep while music of a marching band causes excitement. You do not play a march to put the baby to sleep nor play a lullaby for soldiers marching off to war. Music affects both our physical well-being and our health, it works on our feelings and impacts our emotional state.

Francis Rauscher, Ph.D. of the University of Irvine in California states "that music trains the mind, enhances creativity and develops personality traits." Knowing that music works in a positive way, we also realize that it can also have adverse effects. Parents are often guilty of tuning out their children.

American teenagers listen to approximately 10,500 hours of rock between 7th and 12th grades. This equals 500 hours less than is spent in 12 years of school. Parents need to become involved with the music their children are hearing.

You may be unaware that the recordings which they play over the airwaves are sanitized versions created specifically for radio usage and may not be the lyrics sold to the public. The lyrics may be enclosed in the CD or the tape, but again may not be the same as those recorded. Occasionally, additional songs are included which they do not identify on the package.

Some covers and enclosures are graphic and depict mature themes; yet there are no warnings. Any child can purchase a recording with the explicit lyric label. There are no restrictions unless imposed by the store. Those owners should be commended for their willingness to put our youth before the dollar sign.

Here are some ways to become knowledgeable about popular music:

1. Ask stores if the recordings contain any objectionable material. If purchased and it is unacceptable by your family standards, return the tape or CD and ask for a refund and notify the store manager.

2. Set the example by having other types of music playing on your radio so that young people can learn to appreciate classical, musicals and jazz. Classical music creates a calmer atmosphere.

3. Encourage music lessons. Studies had shown that music lessons improve a child's performance in school. After only eight months of keyboard lessons, preschoolers tested showed a 46% boost in their spatial IQ, which is crucial for higher brain functions. There is a direct correlation between improved test scores and the study of the arts.

4. Check album covers for the parental advisory label, read the lyrics and listen to them with your child. If you are concerned with the message, discuss why it is not acceptable by your standards.

5. Explain to young people the power of music. Use as an example, a horror film. They can just listen to the music with their eyes closed. The music makes the heart beat faster, the palms perspire and the eyes dilate - the body chemistry changes yet they haven't seen a thing. The music has affected their physical and mental state.

6. Be aware of obsessions with certain types of music. Some have themes which can be harmful. Remember that music does not cause unhappiness, but is a reflection of a state of mind. Some messages and performers encourage Satanism and suicide. There are signs which alert the observant parent.

7. Be alert to the music played at school functions - the band, talent shows, dances, and parties. If you overlook the small things they will challenge you the next time by taking it a step further.

The Parents' Music Resource Center is a nonprofit organization funded by private donations which serves as an educational clearinghouse promoting public awareness about the contents of popular music. For further information, please send $1.00 to cover shipping and handling to Parents' Music Resource Center, 1500 Arlington Boulevard, Arlington, VA 22209

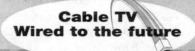

Taking Charge of Your TV

Television has a tremendous influence on our lives. As the dominant force in our media culture, television has changed our habits, what we do with our free time, when and how we eat meals, when we go to bed, and how we raise and entertain our children. Television is an important part of our children's lives, offering them a look at many things they will never have the chance to see for themselves.

Above all else, television teaches. That's why the PTA and the cable industry, concerned about what our children learn from watching television joined forces in 1994 to help parents take control of the family television. In addition to helping parents and educators better understand the effects of television on children, the project teaches critical viewing skills. It shows parents how these skills benefit children in today's media age. The workshops encourage informed choices and participants are given tips and strategies to begin a family dialogue that helps children watch TV actively, carefully and critically.

How much TV to view is a personal choice for every family, but experts tell us the key is to change the way we view television. There are practical ways we can take charge of our children's TV viewing.

Suggestions for Taking Charge of Your Child's TV Viewing

1. Make TV watching a conscious, planned for activity.

Children should ask your permission to watch TV and not be allowed to just casually "channel surf" to see if anything sparks their interest. The simple act of asking gives you the opportunity to respond with a very important one-word question of your own: Why? Each time you do it you'll be reinforcing the principle that "We watch specific shows, not just whatever is on."

Establish family guidelines for selecting programs. Children should know what you value and the reasons for your choices.

Set limits on how much TV your family watches. For example, some experts suggest that preschoolers only view an hour or so a day, and that older children be limited to a maximum of two hours a day. Once you set the right limits for you and your family, stick to them!

Set an example for your children. Make your own TV watching a conscious planned for activity.

Choose programs together

Take time one day each week to review TV program guides for the week ahead. Decide together how your children will "spend" their number of TV viewing hours.

Make TV watching an interactive family event.

Television doesn't have to end family discussion and interaction. Watch it together, and use every opportunity to talk about what you are seeing and hearing. Television can stimulate conversation about topics that can be difficult for some families to discuss, such as feelings about divorce or appropriate sexual behavior.

It's OK to talk back to your TV. Letting your children hear your values — in a nonthreatening way — is useful.

Use TV as a springboard for other learning experiences.

Watching a program on TV can be a useful bridge to reading and other real world activities. TV can create interest in a new topic or idea, thus providing opportunities to learn more about them in other ways. When a topic on TV sparks your child's interest, get to the library or museum and explore the subject further.

During program breaks, ask children what they think might happen next. This helps to develop verbal skills and creative thinking.

Use TV shows to inspire creative expression through drawing or writing. Don't let TV be an excuse for not participating in other activities.

The schedule of TV shows can be a good way for children to learn to tell time. Ask them where the hands of the clock will be when its time for their favorite TV show.

Having your child tell you about a program you missed will help develop valuable communication skills.

For more information on The Family and Community Critical Viewing Project, materials, videos and workshops call 1(800) 743-5355 or write *The Family and Community Critical Viewing Project, 1724 Massachusetts Avenue, NW, Washington, D.C. 20036.*

Your Family TV Viewing Diary

One of the first steps in taking charge of your TV is determining exactly what and how much your family is watching. By using this Family TV Diary, you'll be able to evaluate your family's television viewing habits and decide how they might be changed. Make copies of this page or design your own.

Who Watched	Day/Date	Program Watched	Amount of Time
_____		❑ * _____	_____
_____		❑ * _____	_____
_____		❑ * _____	_____
_____		❑ * _____	_____
_____		❑ * _____	_____
_____		❑ * _____	_____
_____		❑ * _____	_____
_____		❑ * _____	_____
_____		❑ * _____	_____
_____		❑ * _____	_____
_____		❑ * _____	_____
_____		❑ * _____	_____
_____		❑ * _____	_____
_____		❑ * _____	_____
_____		❑ * _____	_____

Check here if program was pre-selected.

Reprinted with permission from
The Family and Community Critical Viewing Project
(800) 743-5355.

Ways to Say "You're Great!"

Good for you!

I'm very proud of you.

I knew you could do it.

You are very good at that.

Good Work!

You're getting better every day.

I like that.

You remembered!

Good Thinking.

You certainly did well today.

Nothing can stop you now!

You've just about mastered that!

You did that well.

Terrific!

Way to go!

You are learning fast.

Good Work!

Well, look at you go!

That's better than ever!

I've never seen anyone do it better!

Surf Safety On the Internet

"Surfing the Net" is a phrase which has become commonplace at work, school and at home. It appears to be innocent. In its truest definition, it is quite innocent and what's more, catchy. But let me take a moment to ask a few questions:

1. Would you allow your children to "surf" or even swim in shark infested waters ?

2. How would you feel if someone purposefully allowed your children to swim in dangerous waters ?

3. How would you feel if you allowed your children to swim in dangerous waters, being naive to the danger which was lurking just under the surface ?

I anticipate your answer and the conviction by which you would give it.

Answers :

1. No Way !!

2. They'd have a law suit on them so fast their heads would swim !!

3. Oh ... If I only knew !!!

This last answer is what we want to address for a moment. *"If I only knew!"*—a statement of tremendous regret usually following devastating circumstances.

Many parents do not understand that "sharks" infest the Internet, seeking whom they can exploit, harm or even devour! Liken to those undersea creatures, whose instinct is to simply feed themselves, there are those whose instinct, however twisted, is to satisfy their hunger. Unfortunately, their hunger involves children. Unfortunately, the Internet has become just another "playground" to search and seize their prey.

The Internet is not a baby sitter and should never be treated as a means to keep your children occupied. Unsupervised, the Internet can lead your child into zones which could be extremely dangerous, emotionally and physically. There is unrestricted access to pornographic and violent content which is readily available and can be found simply using one of many search sites on the net.

Do not depend on "smut blockers" to keep your children out of inappropriate web sites on the network. The best smut blocker only blocks approximately two percent (2%) of available inappropriate content. And if a site happens to be picked up by one of these blockers, the content provider can make their content available and unrestricted within minutes of detection.

A smut blocker will not keep your children from entering network chat rooms or even begin to dialogue with others on the net. These chat rooms are electronic playgrounds by which the art of kidnapping has been taken to a completely new level.

Oh, the techniques are the same. The conversation media is the only thing which has changed and has proven to be even more effective than face to face communications.

Why? Because the face is completely hidden. We've all been taught from childhood not to "speak to strangers." Ask your child what a stranger looks like. You'll be amazed at the answers you will get. The Internet chat room and virtual worlds have removed this element of physical presence by which your child's instinct can assess as to who is dangerous and who is not. You can not hide your age in a face to face encounter. On the net, however, you can pretend to be any age,

from any background and with any interest. This introduces the unique danger of child abuse on the net.

A predator can mask their identity behind any ruse, even to the point of peer level involvement with your child, luring them to believe they are talking with someone with the same age, struggles and questions. Building "virtual" friendships is quite easy these days. Your child is no longer tall or short, thin or stout, excellent or mediocre. The virtual worlds provide a level playing ground, a characteristic of the Internet which is to the advantage of those who would seek your child with unhealthy motives. They simply pretend to be exactly what your child wants them to be.

What's a parent to do? The answer is quite simple—GET INVOLVED!

We know that a parent's influence is still the greatest deterrent to a child's behavioral disposition. Simply take that influence into this particular topic. You must be keenly aware of what content is of interest to your child. You must help your child find that particular content on the Internet. You must take an interest in your child's adventures on the net. You must always be watching over their shoulder to ensure that they are not surfing in shark infested waters.

Ask questions like:

1. What sites do you normally visit?

2. Have you developed any friendships while in the chat room?

3. What is your new friend's interests?

4. Has your new friend given you their e-mail address?

5. Do you write to them often ?

6. Has your friend told you their age, school they go to, address, etc.?

7. Has your new friend ever asked to meet you some-where?

If you understand where we are going with these questions, then you are ahead of the game and are now beginning to understand that you must never allow your child's access to the Internet to become totally unrestricted; using your personal or home account, at school or even over a friend's house. Identify every access point to the net which is at the disposal to your child. Talk to the authority of that access point, ask questions, set strategies and set rules with your child.

In short, Be involved!! You, the parent, represent the shark cage which allows your child to enjoy the wonders of the deep, without the threat of shark's teeth.

If you are still not convinced, then go to your favorite search site and look up the word ... sex

---

H. Mike Rice
(301) 893-0012
mrice@vidtel.com

The Kite

When I was a little boy, Vietnam was at war with France. My family joined a resistance village in the rain forest. There, life was hard and I did not have any toys. One day, my father cut down a bamboo tree to make me a big bow-shaped kite. He dipped the kite in a lotus pond for the entire night. Then he let if dry in the hot sun until its wings became brown and tautly stretched. Together, we brought it to the windy bank and watched it soar.

That was the first of many wonderful afternoons I spent with my father. He delighted me with stories of the serene days before the war broke out. He spoke of kites as big as houses and so powerful they had to be restrained by dozens of grown men during the village festivals. He filled me with the joyful vision of kites of all shapes and colors darting swiftly in the wind like magnificent dragons in a mythical world.

For us, life was not so easy. At the faintest droning of an airplane, we would hurriedly take the kite down and run for cover in the dense foliage. But, despite all the danger and hardship, I never felt happier. By taking the time to fly that kite, my father let me know that he loved me.

As I grew up, Vietnam was engulfed in another, even larger war. Thousands of people were forced into exile abroad. I moved to Houston, Texas. There was emptiness in my heart.

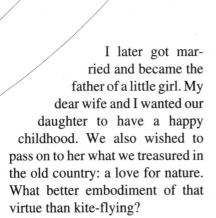

Hence, under fluttering kites, my family often savored together the wonders of rushing winds, whispering leaves and ever-changing clouds. We also spent long hours talking with one another. These moments of togetherness bond us with joyful, invisible ties. Watching my daughter experience the same happiness I once shared with my father made the emptiness in my heart go away.

My father died when he was very young, so I did not have the chance to know him well. Somehow, the time we spent together at the windy river bank is etched in my memory. The kite he gave me so long ago still flutters inside me. Like a tireless traveler across time and space, it delivers a message from one generation to the next- life can be hard, but love will sweeten it. O winds of the big sky, fly our kites high!

I later got married and became the father of a little girl. My dear wife and I wanted our daughter to have a happy childhood. We also wished to pass on to her what we treasured in the old country: a love for nature. What better embodiment of that virtue than kite-flying?

Andy Vu

notes

notes

HELPING YOUR TEEN SUCCEED

I Don't Have Time To Read, Honest! 108
ERIC

Talking with Your Adolescent About School 110
Center for Early Adolescence

**What to Look For In a School Environment
for Young Adolescents** 112

Ways to Say "You're Great" 115
Anonymous

Keeping Your Children Safe From Drugs 118

Giving Your Teen the Rights to The Road 121
Phil Berardelli

How Good A Listener Are You? 124

Teens and Money 126
Blaine Harris

Steps to Planning for College 128
U. S. Department of Education

Finding Financial Aid For College 130
U. S. Department of Education

I Don't Have Time to Read– Honest!

An amazing thing happens to children: they grow into adulthood. In the time of greatest change, teenagers can look like adults and act like children (and vice versa). The transformation is wonderful, and, at times, frightening.

The unpredictable behavior of adolescence can weaken the relationship between parent and child. That's too bad, because the process leading into adulthood is what the word "education" originally meant (in Latin). If we abandon teenagers to their own devices, we abandon their education.

Take reading. In childhood, the stress is to learn to read. When our children do learn, we are apt to sigh in relief. School success is clearly a lot easier when a child reads well. Later, however, we take less interest in our teenagers' reading habits. Perhaps we think, "let them relax and watch TV or gab on the phone."

When that happens, we've lost it. Because reading isn't some kind of chore, and teenagers don't need to get the message that it is. Reading with a purpose is part of the adult role. The idea of purpose is a bit complicated, but it means that the adult has some reason—some motive that he or she is aware of—for reading. There are about as many motives as there are adults, so "motivation" is not really a problem.

Parents and teachers can help teenagers discover those motives. Obviously, that can happen only when adults who read actively share experiences, views, and information with the teenagers they care about. Teenagers seek role models, and both parents and teachers are near at hand for this purpose—so becoming a role model is not really so difficult.

Some motives that have meaning for teenagers include knowledge about personal relationships and getting insights into one's own identity. They include reading that helps a person develop opinions and values or understand current events. More practical motives include investigating career options, expanding knowledge of a hobby or special interest, or becoming a more shrewd shopper.

When people who care about them read and share the importance of reading, then teenagers learn not just how to read, but they learn the reason for reading.

Staff of ERIC/CRESS prepared this article, based on information in the ERIC database. (800) USE-ERIC.

Talking with Your Adolescent about School

Your child just entered adolescence and everything seems to change. Overnight, the way your young adolescent talks about school is quite different. The once bubbling, wide-eyed accounts of the day's events in school are replaced by a wider variety of responses, ranging from excited descriptions to mere grunts. Why does a small difference in age make such a great difference in the way youngsters talk about school?

Adolescence Brings Change

Young people, parents and schools change as children reach adolescence. Most 10 to 15- year olds attend junior and middle schools that are larger, more impersonal, and probably more complex than the elementary schools they came from. Often, they have several teachers, each with different standards and expectations. Their relationships with their families and their friends alter as they grow physically and develop new interests.

With all these changes taking place, it is not surprising that parents sometimes find it difficult to talk to their young teenagers about school. However, the newly developing ability to think abstractly, coupled with the emergence of keen observational skills, can make communication easier and more fun with young adolescents. If parents are willing to accept the changes in their children and to listen to their concerns, talking about school should be a pleasant experience.

Importance of School for Young Adolescents

Parents often see school solely as a place for their young adolescents to learn the skills necessary for further education and future employment. Young adolescents see school as much more than a place to learn facts and skills. Many significant experiences in a young adolescent's life take place in school. They do not just go to school; they live at school six or seven hours a day.

What Parents Want and Need to Know . . . and How to Ask

Parents usually want to know if their youngsters are safe, if they are working up to their capacity, and whether the school is a "good" school. In addition, parents need to know if the school provides a healthy environment for their children. Does the school actively consider the needs for its young adolescent students? Here are some things to consider:

Does the school provide:

• Diverse learning experiences and relationships?

• Opportunities for self-exploration and self-discovery?

• Opportunity for students to participate in a meaningful way in their school and community?

• Positive social interaction among students and between students and staff?

• Opportunities for physical activity?

• Opportunities for students to be successful and feel competent, especially in the basic subjects?

• Appropriate structure and clear limits?

Discussing school not only gives you information about your child's education, it also can strengthen your relationship. How, then can you get past the "yes" and "no" answers, the questions about homework, and the one-way lectures about the importance of school to really talk about your adolescent's school experience? Here are some questions you can ask:

____Is there something you are especially good at that you get to do at school?

____Is the work too hard, too easy, or just right for you?

____Do you have a close relationship with an adult staff member?

____What are the three most important school rules?

____What happens when one of the three most important rules is broken?

____Do you think the rules are fair or reasonable? Why or why not?

____Do students have a voice in making decisions and establishing rules at school? How?

____Do you worry a lot about having things stolen from you or your safety at school?

____What changes would you like to see at your school?

Adapted from *Talking with Young Adolescents about School*, Center for Early Adolescence, School of Medicine, University of North Carolina at Chapel Hill, Suite D-2, Carr Mill Town Center, Carrboro, NC 27510 (919) 966-1148

What to Look for in a School Environment for Young Adolescents

Successful schools for young adolescents have created healthy environments where students learn the "basics," learn how to think for themselves, have opportunities to succeed in a variety of ways, learn about themselves and others, and enjoy school and learning. You can help your young adolescent and your school create such as environment by being informed and involved in the school.

There are many successful schools for young adolescents across our country. These schools share some common characteristics that you may want to look for in your child's school:

Leadership:

- The principal is the instructional leader of the school.

- There is a philosophy or statement of purpose which is generally accepted by the school staff, the students, and the parents.

Use of physical space:

- The building is neat, clean, and in good repair.

- Student work is displayed throughout the building.

- There are few, if any graffiti in the school. This is a measure of school pride and student acceptance of school rules.

Use of human resources:

- Students are meaningfully involved in decision making. They make significant contributions to the school.

- Parents are involved in the school and in their child's education.

- All staff members are responsible for all students. Inappropriate behavior is dealt with whenever and wherever it occurs.

- Teachers and staff are visible outside classrooms and offices. They are seen chatting or playing informally with students during breaks.

Social and emotional environment:

- The school is safe for students and staff.

- Every student has a close relationship with at least one adult in the school.

- Staff express fondness for the age group.

- Staff members do not belittle students in front of other staff or students.

- Students and staff enjoy being at the school. Their vitality and high interest are evident.

- Absentee rates among students and staff are low.

Programming:

- The community is involved is the life of the school.

- There is an accepted, well understood approach to discipline.

- The suspension rate is low.

- Guidance is seen as a shared responsibility.

Activities for Teens 12-16

Television can offer you and your teenager a springboard for discussing important issues and events during a difficult time when conversation is not always easy.

1. Ask your teenager's opinion about a particular program. Also, ask: what would you do in this situation? Do you know anyone who has had this experience?

2. Have your teenagers watch for stereotypes of women as sexy but dumb; men as tough and not sensitive; older people as feeble or helpless.

3. Find a story in the news that interests your teen and compare the story as it's presented on TV, in the newspaper or in a news magazine.

4. Talk about whom advertisers are trying to reach. Have them figure out who the "target audience" is, based on what products are advertised during a given show.

5. After a violent program, talk about the consequences of violence. Ask your teen to predict what would happen to the victim and the victim's family in real life. What happens to the criminal and his family after they catch the criminal?

Help Wanted

Older students are interested in life beyond school. You can help them have a realistic sense of what's out there.

What you'll need

Pen or pencil
Paper
Newspaper "help wanted" ads
Friends and neighbors

What to do

Talk with your child: "What job do you think you would like to do when you get out of school? What training do you think you will need to get this job?"

Suggest that your child pick two adults he or she knows, such as neighbors or relatives, to interview briefly about their jobs.

Help your child think of at least three questions to write down, leaving space for the answers. Sample questions: What is your job? How long have you held it? What kind of special training did you need? Have your child do the interviews. (You may want to help him or her get started.) After the interview, talk about what your child learned. Now your child will be more comfortable doing the next step.

Read a page of the newspaper help wanted ads together. Have your child find ads for three jobs that he or she might want in the future. Talk together about the training needed for each job: Can they learn some of it on the job? How much schooling is necessary?

Have your child find people who already have these jobs and interview them.

Remember that there will be many new kinds of jobs in the future.

What children—and adults, too— need to do is be flexible and keep learning.

Give your kids the world.

Technology offers today's children more learning opportunities than previous generations ever imagined. Take the Internet, for example. It enables kids to learn about the world in ways never before possible. And puts the knowledge of the universe at their fingertips. You can help your children get the most out of the Internet with the following tips:

- To save time, learn to use search engines effectively and bookmark your family's favorite sites.
- Always preview any sites you intend to share with your children.
- Although it's best to supervise your kids on the Internet, you might also consider using software that restricts access to inappropriate sites when you're not there.

A Special Offer From EDS

To register your child for a chance to win *one year of free Internet access,* call 888-607-7566. Just leave your name, phone number and your child's name. No purchase required. A new winner will be named each month from 6/98 through 6/99. Only one entry per child per month, please.

EDS

"The first and most basic element in effective parenting is a healthy environment. Vitally related to this is the church/faith community. Commitment to nurturing relationships, establishment of spiritual, mental, physical, social, emotional renewal are critical means for surviving parental crisis. Valuing the Church and its significance in structuring a healthy environment may well be the crowning achievement in effective parenting."

Rev. Lee P. Washington, Ph.D.
Reid Temple A.M.E. Church
Lanham, Maryland

Keeping the Peace Begins at Home . . .

Keeping a peaceful environment is not always easy. It can be very challenging Orange County Department of Education offers these tips:

Set some ground rules. You may want to try the following:

1. Agree to solve the problem

2. Talk one at a time

3. No name calling or put downs

4. Be honest

Reprinted from Keeping the Peace: A Conflict Resolution Guide for Parents. Orange County Department of Education. Keeping the Peace video equips parents and children with a model of conflict resolution that stresses positive solutions to everyday problems. It shows how to overcome struggles within the family, explains how verbal and listening skills contribute to understanding and resolve and provides resource information to help parents deal with issues of prejudice and discrimination. It can be used as a resource by parents, schools, and organizations. For more information contact: Orange County Department of Education, Media Services Unit, 200 Kalmus Drive, Costa Mesa, CA 92626 or E-Mail: education–materials@ocde.k12.ca.us. (800) 414-5844 (United States Only) or (714) 966-4341

Keeping Your Children Safe From Drugs

It is vitally important for parents to learn about the affects of drugs and to recognize the signs of drug use. This knowledge can be used to guide youngsters and help them acquire the strength to resist peer pressure to use drugs. Strong family support and firm, caring direction are necessary to help children develop confidence and to acquire a balanced sense of personal values. Tell your children you love them, accept them as they are, not as you think they should be. Encouragement and praise can help children develop faith in themselves.

Talk to your children about their interests and problems. Be able to discuss drugs knowledgeably. Listen carefully when your children are talking, give attention and avoid interrupting. Allow your child to express and share his/her views, this is the only way you can hope to know what's going on in their lives. Accepting their feelings doesn't mean you are condoning habits or attitudes. Impress on the child that drugs are not cool nor acceptable, in fact, just the opposite is true. Drugs taken illegally and improperly are hazardous to health and often deadly. Parents should set a good example by not using drugs themselves.

Three simple steps you can take:

* Discuss household rules regarding drug use and then strictly apply.

* Clearly outline limits and behavioral standards

* Support teachers and administrators who are tough on drugs. Encourage the development of a school policy with a strong no drug message.

Signs of Drug Abuse

Parents should be aware of changing patterns of behavior, appearance and performance which may indicate a problem associated with drug or alcohol use. Some of these signs are: distinct personality changes, starting to use foul language, changes in friends, lowered school grades, violent behavior and fits of anger, sloppy dress, changes in sleeping or eating habits, money or valuables missing from the house, increasing dishonesty, smell of alcohol or marijuana, drug paraphernalia, or empty bottles hidden in bedroom, truancy from school, and deteriorating family relationships. Some of these changes are part of the adolescent stage, but enough of them should raise the suspicion of chemical abuse.

Care must be taken not to falsely accuse. Parents who suspect drug use must deal with their own emotions or anger and guilt. To deny the signs and postpone confronting the child allows the problem to become worse. Instead obtain sufficient facts, and then approach the suspected drug abuser in a firm but rational manner. Do not confront a child while he/she is under the influence of drugs. If warranted seek professional help.

Responses to Avoid:

When dealing with a drug-abuse situation at home, the accusatory approach, "You're lying to me." only puts the child on the defensive and blocks further talk between parent and child. Likewise, statements such as, "Don't think for one minute you can hide what you are doing from me," or saying, "How could you do such a terrible thing?" are examples of how to widen the communications gap between parent and child.

When a child is made to feel defensive and excluded from the family, that feeling often translates into drug abuse. Open and regular communication among family members is vital to growth and understanding.

Self-reproach should be avoided as well. There is no point in asking yourself or your child, "Where have I gone wrong?" Start making positive changes now. What is past cannot be changed, but today can be improved by all of us if we become more positive, aware, informed, alert, and confident.

Reprinted from the forthcoming book, *Drugs of Abuse Digest,* Education First Foundation

---

Teach your teens the ABCs of responsible driving.

Drivers and passengers must wear safety belts.

Drive defensively – watch out for the other guy.

Never drive or ride with anyone under the influence of drugs or alcohol.

Kids learn life's most valuable lessons from their parents. Which is why at GEICO we encourage parents to play an active role in teaching teens about "road responsibility." But talk isn't enough. Because driving habits are best taught by example. And, down the road, you may save more than just a few bucks on your next car insurance bill.

Giving Your Teen the Rights to the Road

Is Your Child Ready to Drive?

Too many children are harmed because they simply do not understand how much power they are attempting to control when they get behind the wheel. Or, they have not been trained properly so they put themselves into situations that they cannot overcome when things go wrong. Or, as so many kids do, they believe they cannot be harmed, so despite the skills they have learned they risk themselves - and sometimes their passengers.

Most of the time, nothing happens, but when something does, either it's too late to help or the young driver's skills are insufficient. Usually, it's both. Good driving habits are very easy to learn. They must be practiced, over and over. They must be accompanied by good judgment, which also takes time to develop.

Driving skills cannot be used properly unless they are reflexive. You can't think about evasive actions while you're executing them. It takes too long. When needed, skills must be automatic. And they can only become automatic by practicing them, over and over. There is no other way.

Think of playing a musical instrument. You can't sit down at the piano and perform like an expert right away. It takes time to read the music, to learn the technique, to strengthen the muscles guiding the hands and the fingers, to develop senses of rhythm and emphasis. When you learn to play a melody, you no longer think about the individual notes. Instead, your fingers feel the sequence. They move faster than you can think. The skill that is displayed by playing well is performed by a different part of the brain than conscious thinking.

Driving is no different. If you had to think about everything you were doing, you would be constantly tense. You would quickly become fatigued. For example, whenever you drive through thick fog, rain, or snow, especially at night, you tend to search every foot of the road almost frantically for a sudden obstruction or change. Time seems to slow down. It takes forever to go anywhere. Your muscles tense. Your heart rate elevates. You have a general feeling of unease. After a brief time, you become tired.

On the other hand, if the weather is clear and visibility is good, especially on a roadway frequently traveled, you are at ease. You don't exert conscious effort. Just like playing a well-practiced tune on the piano, driving is performed automatically. It's second nature.

With this in mind, I argue that it's impossible for someone who has just turned sixteen to have good driving skills. There has not been enough time for those skills to appear. And if a teenager doesn't have good skills, what is he or she doing on the road? This is why I believe all parents must decide, not whether their child is ready to drive at sixteen, but whether the child is ready to learn to drive.

Setting Sensible Limits:

Teens will need to gain still more experience on the road before being permitted to go anywhere they please, whenever they please. This isn't just personal opinion. More and more states are enacting or considering graduated driving programs for teens with strong

support from insurance companies and parent organizations. These programs are meant to place reasonable limits on driving privileges for minors.

Even if such limits don't exist in your state or locality, you should nevertheless consider imposing them, especially during the first few months of the license. For instance:

No driving over 55.

No passing on high-speed two lane blacktop.

No high-speed heavy traffic.

No driving after midnight (and perhaps earlier on school nights).

No passengers.

It goes without saying, no drugs or alcohol. And seat belts are a requirement at all times.

Post-License Checkups:

Once they obtain the license, it's important to give your teen some time to develop. All the material learned in the lessons must be practiced continuously. Even with the limits, there should be plenty of opportunities to drive solo during the first year.

It is very easy to keep track of your teen's progress. Allow your teen to drive you anytime you need to go somewhere. This will allow you to observe, continue to teach and to compliment things that are performed well. You also should let your teen drive on long trips. It's beneficial for both of you. It breaks up the monotony of the journey, and it's valuable experience for the novice driver. Try alternating every two hours, with a five-or ten-minute break in between. Two hours is about as long as anybody can drive nonstop without fatigue setting in. Stopping for short breaks at two-hour intervals is a very good habit to instill.

Excerpted from SAFE YOUNG DRIVERS©, Phil Berardelli. Phil has been a writer and journalist for over 25 years, covering such topics as energy, education and popular culture. His work appears in *The Washington Post, Los Angeles Times, Pittsburgh Post-Gazette* and other newspapers and magazines.

He was a middle school teacher for seven years. For five years, he produced and co-hosted the weekly television program, "The Moviegoing Family," which appeared in the Washington, D.C. area and nationally on The Learning Channel. Copies of *Safe Young Drivers* can be obtained from EPM Publications, Inc., McLean, Virginia at a cost of $12.00. For more information or to order a copy call (800) 289-2339

For information on drinking and driving contact Washington Regional Alcohol Program (WRAP) at (703) 893–0461.

How Good a Listener Are You?

These questions are intended to stimulate your thinking about your listening skills. Check the response which most honestly describes your behavior.

1. Were members of your family good listeners?   Yes____ No____

2. Do you have a tendency to interrupt family or friends when they are speaking?   Yes____ No____

3. Do you tend to tune certain people out when they are talking to you?   Yes____ No____

4. Do you tune out your children more frequently than you do adults?   Yes____ No____

5. Do you pay more attention to your children when they are bad than when they are good?   Yes____ No____

6. Have you had a lengthy heart-to-heart talk with any of your children in the last six months?   Yes____ No____

7. Have your children had the opportunity to talk with you at any length about themselves or their lives lately?   Yes____ No____

8. Can your children count on your having 15 minutes each day to talk to them without distractions or interruptions?   Yes____ No____

9. Do you usually do other things while "listening" to your children?   Yes____ No____

10. Do you maintain direct eye contact with your children when they speak to you?   Yes____ No____

11. Do you frequently look at your watch when
    your children are talking?   Yes____ No____

12. Do you listen more carefully to one of your
    children more than another?   Yes____ No____

13. Have you made an audio recording or videotape
    of your interactions with your children and
    carefully reviewed it?   Yes____ No____

14. Have your listening skills improved since
    you were a teenager?   Yes____ No____

15. Would your children agree with your
    responses to these questions?   Yes____ No____

16. Do your children consider you a
    "good listener"?   Yes____ No____

Teens and Money

Older children should have a portion of all the money they have earned or received available to them to use in any way they want. As a parent, you can counsel them on what you think might be the best purchase, but sometimes letting them make a poor purchasing choice at this stage in life is the best lesson they could ever learn on how to spend. Once they have made the decision, let them live with it. If they see something else two weeks later that they really want, let them know they must save their money to buy it - don't lend them the money and let them pay it back. If there is an occasion where you feel you should "lend" your child some money, make sure when it is paid back it is with interest so the child can learn the cost of borrowing.

Children of all ages need to understand, if they do not have the money available, they do not have the money to purchase the item they are wanting. Going into debt should not happen. Teaching children how to control impulse buying and how to evaluate the value of a purchase prior to making it is invaluable behavior that will serve them well throughout their lives and literally by putting dollars in their pocket.

It is good to understand the principle of "give some, save some, invest some and spend some". Here are some general guidelines and limits. You may want to modify the percentages to meet your particular family's needs.

"Give some" - Charity 10% - teaching generosity is an important principle that may be lacking today. Let your child personally give 10 cents of each dollar to a church, school library or community project. It is possible to be generous and wise with money and the principle spills over into how they use and manage other resources such as time and talents in every day life.

"Save some" - Short term savings 30% - saving for things such as clothing, a car, anything that has merit but requires a pool of money to purchase. For younger children this may even be used for a very elaborate toy or special item.

"Invest some" - Long term savings 30% - saving for college, marriage or other special long term needs. As a parent you may even want to match everything that is put into a long term savings program. If you put $1,000 into an investment at the time of your child's birth and it was left to accrue at a rate of return averaging 12% per year until the child was 67, your child would have nearly $2 million dollars or $40,000 per year at retirement. Waiting until the child is 6 to do the same thing cuts the amount in half, but half is better than nothing.

"Spend some" - Discretionary spending money 30% - let your children enjoy the fruits of their labor. Help them set goals and get used to making decisions about spending. Learning how to spend is as important as learning how to save. Ironically, when we learn how to spend properly our savings increases at a more rapid pace.

Teaching our children healthy views toward money is essential. Too much emphasis may make them think the only thing in life that is important is money; too little focus and they may succumb to the pitfalls of financial mismanagement that will plague every aspect of their adult lives. Helping children create a balance when it comes to personal money management will reward them many times over. Remember, teaching your children how to manage and use money through your own good example and hands on learning is a greater gift than giving them money itself.

Based on a true story, Blaine Harris's book, *The Four Laws of Debt Free Prosperity*, tells the fascinating story of one lady's financial experiences. By the time you finish reading her story of going from extreme debt to extreme prosperity, you will have learned the Four Laws which are, Track, Target, Trim, and Train. These laws can be applied in any home or business and by any family, parent or child, resulting in the debt free prosperity we all desire for ourselves and our families.

Steps to Planning for College

8th and 9th Grades

1. Find out which courses to take in high school to prepare academically for college. Performance in high school can play an important part in gaining admission to college.

2. Save money now to pay for school if you haven't already done so.

10th Grade

1. Think about selecting a school. Find out about the different types of schools, and decide which characteristics of schools are most important to your student.

2. Prepare for school entrance exams. Take the PSAT now in preparation for next year.

11th Grade

1. Gather information from schools. Write for brochures and catalogs, attend college fairs, and begin college visits.

2. Retake the PSAT for a shot at a National Merit Scholarship, and take the SAT and ACT in the spring.

12th Grade

1. Finish gathering information on schools, select four to six you like best, and apply for admission. Retake the SAT and ACT if you aren't satisfied with your first results.

2. Apply for financial aid by filling out the Free Application for Federal Student Assistance. Consider all of your options for paying for school. Find out about scholarships and grants before taking out a student loan.

Higher Education Planning Checklist

✓ Save money as early as possible to help pay for your child's education.

✓ Encourage your child to take classes in high school that will academically prepare him or her for higher education.

✓ Discuss with your child his or her skills and interests, career options and schools he or she is interested in attending.

✓ Meet with the high school guidance counselor to determine what schools match your child's academic abilities.

✓ Gather information about the schools your child is interested in attending including information on financial aid.

✓ Help your child apply for admission. To apply for financial aid, help your child complete the Free Application for Federal Student Aid.

✓ Consider scholarships, grants, loans and work-study programs.

✓ Complete any necessary applications or forms. Consider loans only after you have researched all the sources of free financial aid.

✓ Consider the loan programs available to you and your child. Federal loan programs include Federal Family Education Loans, Federal Direct Loans, and Federal Perkins Loans.

✓ Help your child to manage his or her student loan debt by deciding how much you and your child can afford to borrow and repay.

Finding Financial Aid for College

The Student Guide is the most comprehensive resource on student aid from the U.S. Department of Education. Grants, loans, and work-study are the three major forms of student financial aid available through the federal Student Financial Assistance Programs. The Student Guide is updated each award year. It tells you about programs and how to apply for them.

To apply for federal financial aid, and state student aid programs, students must complete a Free Application for Federal Student Aid (FAFSA).

For additional information, contact the high school guidance counselor, the financial aid officer at the postsecondary institution your student plans to attend, or the Federal Student Aid Information Center. The Information Center is open Monday through Friday, from 8 a.m. to 8 p.m. (Eastern Time). (800) 4 FED-AID

Federal Aid Quick Summary

Pell Grants

- For undergraduates only

- Grant: No repayment

- Students must have Expected Family Contribution of $2100 or less

- Maximum award $2300

- Deadline is May 2, at the END of the school year for which aid is sought

- Students paid directly or school account is credited

Supplemental Education Opportunity Grants "(SEOG)

- For undergraduates only

- Grant: No repayment

- For students with exceptional financial need

- Maximum award $4,000 (may vary by school)

- Deadline set by school

- Students paid directly or school account is credited

Federal Work–Study (FWS)

- For both undergraduates and graduates

- Undergraduates can receive aid for more than one degree

- Provides jobs both on-campus and off-campus

- Amount earned can't exceed your financial need

- Amount dependent on funds available at each school

- Deadline set by school

- Undergraduates paid by the hour, graduates paid by salary or hourly

- All students paid at least monthly

Perkins Loans

- For both undergraduates and graduates

- Undergraduates can receive aid for more than one degree

- For students with exceptional financial need

- Deadline set by school

- Interest rate: 5%

- Students must sign a promissory note, agreeing to repay

Stafford Loans

- For undergraduates and graduates enrolled at least half-time

- Loans available regardless of income, but federal government pays interest while in school on need-based loans

- Loans made by lender (bank/credit union), guaranteed by government; or can be direct loan from government

- Interest rate: Variable up to 8.25%

- Students must sign a promissory note, agreeing to repay

- Under certain conditions, repayment may be postponed or canceled

Parent Loans for Undergraduate Students (PLUS)

- For parents of dependent undergraduates

- Loans available regardless of income; credit check required

- Loans made by lender (bank/credit union), guaranteed by government

- Interest rate: Variable up to 9%

- Parents must sign a promissory note, agreeing to repay

- Maximum award is cost of education minus other aid received

notes

notes

You Are Not Alone!

Unity 136
Author Unknown

A Family Friendly Corporation 137
Norma Anderson

Resources 140

Join The Partnership 148

AEL 151

Hand-in-Hand 152

NPDC 153

Parental Involvement Pledge 157

Unity

I dreamed I stood in a studio

And watched two sculptors there

The clay they used was a young child's mind

And they fashioned it with care.

One was a teacher - the tools he used,

Were books, music, and art.

The other, a parent, worked with a guiding hand,

And a gentle heart.

Day after day, the teacher toiled with touch

That was deft and sure,

While the parent labored by his side

And polished and smoothed it o'er.

And when at last their task was done

They were proud of what they had wrought,

For the things they had molded into the child

Could neither be sold nor bought.

And each agreed they would have failed

If each had worked alone.

For behind the teacher stood the school

And behind the parent, the home.

Author Unknown

A Family Friendly Corporation

In order for parents to fully participate in their child's education, they must have the support of the family, friends, the community and their place of employment. The following story, excerpted from a speech presented to American Association of University Women by Norma Anderson, Vice President, Development Resources, Ceridian Corporation, demonstrates what major corporations are doing to help families. Ceridian Corporation was awarded the National Parents' Day Coalition 1997-98 Vanguard Award for its progressive workplace policies and programs benefiting and supporting families.

On a Saturday night not long ago in a hotel room in a distant city, a Ceridian employee on a business trip sat down to write our C.E.O. a letter. That it was a Saturday night is significant. The weekend is family time. And, not quite coincidentally, the cheapest airfares require a stay over Saturday night. Our employee had concluded his business and was ready to come home. But, as he explained in his letter, he was expected to stay over Saturday night to save a few hundred dollars for the company. There he sat alone while his family spent the weekend without him. It was not a dramatic letter, but it was a sad one. And it very much reflects outmoded tradition. Let me tell you about the response to that letter.

But first, let's take a closer look at tradition. Doing things the old way, work was work and home was home and never the twain should meet. If a conflict arose, it was understood that home life would suffer, that family had to take the back seat. The merest mention of family needs might be judged to show evidence of lack of commitment to the job. A serious, ambitious employee very much needed a supportive family to back him up and sustain him. I use the male pronoun advisedly. Such an employee very nearly required a stay–at–home wife.

Proof of that has come in recent years, as women have entered the workforce in record numbers. When mom is no longer at home all day, the family/work conflict is forced to the surface. As mothers, wives, sisters, and daughters, women still tend to carry a disproportionate share of the load of family care. The reasons for this are worth pondering. And companies with family-friendly cultures will, I hope, help move us toward a future of gender fairness in sharing these responsibilities.

Meanwhile, women are now in the workforce and family needs keep coming. Johnny is sent home sick from school. Suzy has a parent/ teacher conference at one in the afternoon. Grandma needs someone to take her to the dentist at ten. Uncle Henry's back is out and he's got to have groceries. How is it all going to get done?

Some of these needs must be attended to during working hours. It is no longer possible to hide these responsibilities from the employer, if mom is on the job, or if dad is a single parent, or ... there are so many possibilities. Families come in so many configurations these days. The old family structure that could bow and bend to the requirements of the workplace and keep out of sight, has gone the way of the dinosaur.

The Ceridian employee in his lonely hotel room, separated from family over Saturday night, might well be a single father, or a son with aging parents to care for. He might well be a member of a nontraditional family, a very much needed member. And he very likely needs his family, as well. If he is a successful person, he probably has a life.

When Ceridian focused on family/ work balance, in order to become a better place to work and a stronger, more profitable company as a result, we had to turn tradition aside. We had to start fresh to discover who we are, how our families function, and what they require.

A family-friendly company takes the employee into account as a whole person, including the responsibilities he or she may be balancing with work duties. In a family-friendly corporation, there's the understanding that addressing family issues is not in conflict, but congruent with business needs. An employee who is assisted and not hindered in meeting family responsibilities will be a more productive, creative employee.

We need new definitions. And this process of redefinition is ongoing.

Let's return to our Ceridian employee alone in his hotel room on Saturday night, his business concluded the day before. Ceridian has no explicit policy on the matter. Employees were never officially required to stay over Saturdays to save the company money. Employees were never officially instructed that they could return once business was concluded.

But the employee's letter brought the matter to light. And in response, our C.E.O., Larry Perlman, who is a champion of family issues in the workplace and sits on the Families and Work Institute Board of Directors, sent out a message to managers, reminding them of Ceridian's commitment to family and asking them not to require traveling employees to stay overnight Saturdays unless essential for conducting business. Of course, it sometimes happens that employees stay over Saturday night because it suits their plans. It's nice when an employee's needs and the company needs coincide. The point is that the company recognized the employee as a whole person and honored the weekend as family and personal time.

That he had to write the letter shows how far we have to go. That he wrote it shows that we're moving in the right direction. There is no automatic conflict between the aims and needs of the workplace and those of personal and family life. With creativity and thought, the two can work together, can be woven together in partnership.

Norma Anderson is the Vice President of Development Resources for Ceridian Corporation (previously Control Data Corporation). In her position, Norma is responsible for Ceridian's diversity effort, including work family initiatives, as well as, affirmative action programs, and corporation contributions.

Resources on Parent/Family Involvement

American Association of School Administrators
1801 North Moore Street
Arlington, VA 22209
(703) 875-0730
Request *101 Ways Parents Can Help Students Achieve; What to Do If ... A Guide for Parents of Teenagers; and Parents... Partners in Education.*

American Federation of Teachers
555 North Jersey Avenue NW
Washington, DC 20001
Request *Home Team: Learning Activities*

Appalachia Educational Laboratory
Family Connections
P.O. Box 1348
Charleston, WV 25325
Call toll free (800) 624-9120
Request *information on the Family Connections guides*

Aspira Association, Inc.
1112 16th Street, NW, Suite 340
Washington, DC 20036
(202) 835-3600
Request *a catalog of material in Spanish*

Family Involvement Partnership for Learning
U.S. Department of Education
Washington, DC 20202
(800) USA-LEARN

Home-School Institute, Inc.
Special Projects Office
1500 Mass. Ave., NW
Washington, DC 20036
(202) 466-3633

National Association for the Education of Young Children NAEYC)
1834 Connecticut Avenue, NW
Washington, DC 20009-2460
Call toll free (800) 424-2460

National Black Child Development Institute
1023 15ᵗʰ Street, NW, Suite 600
Washington, DC 20005
(202) 387-1281
Request *African-American Family Reading List and a catalog*

National Coalition for Parent Involvement in Education
1001 Connecticut Avenue, NW
Washington, DC 20036
(202) 822-8405
Request *Guide to Parent Involvement Resources*

National Head Start Association
1651 Prince Street
Alexandria, VA 22314
(703) 739-0875

National Parent Information Network (NPIN)
ERIC/CUE
Teachers College Box 40
Columbia University
New York, NY 10027
(800) 601-4868

Family-Friendly Places on the NET

✦ The Franklin Institute Science Museum http://sln.fi.edu/ offers online exhibits on an array of science and technology topics.

✦ Find good books to read, including Newbery and Caldecott Award Winners, at the American Library Association site http://www.ala.org/parents/index.html. This site includes information about authors, KidsConnect (for help locating all the information online), and educational games.

✦ Watch "Live from Mars," audio and video transmissions of the Pathfinder's explorations, at NASA's Quest Project site http://guest.arc.nasa.gov. Find more adventures in space, including views from the Hubble Space Telescope, at a different NASA site http://spacelink.nasa.gov.

✦ Climb Mt. Everest, explore inside the Pyramids, and go on other electronic field trips with the Public Broadcasting System at http://www.pbs.org/. Preschool children can enjoy children's programming here, elementary school children can practice story telling, and teenagers and adults can take telecourses.

✦ Join an interactive exploration of the oceans, on the earth and beyond, with the Jason Project http://jasonproject.org.

✦ Puzzle over optical illusions, take memory tests, and conduct experiments, online and off, at the Exploratorium http://www.exploratorium.edu.

✦ Enjoy materials from the Library of Congress http://www.loc.gov, including exhibits on topics ranging from ballet to Jelly Roll Morton, Native American flutes to Thomas Jefferson's pasta machine.

✦ Read stories with your children, let then add to the stories told around the Global Campfire, and find links to other good family sites at Parents and Children Together Online http://www.indiana.edu/~ericrec/fl/pcto/menu.html.

✦ Get educational resources through distance learning from Healthlinks http://www.mcwt.edu/healthlinks/index.html.

✦ Find information on blocking software from Netparents at http://www.netparents.org.

✦ Try the Air Force's new family-friends site for kids at http://www.af.mil/aflinkir.

✦ "50+ Great Site for Kids and Parents," from the American Library Association (ALA) enables preschool through elementary school children to explore rainbows, black history, castles for kids, award-winning news reported by children for children, the Kids Web Page Hall of Fame, to say nothing of watching dolphins, learning lullabies, and much more http://www.ssdesign.com/parentspage/greatsites/50.html.

✦ Jean Armour Polly's "Fifty Extraordinary Experiences for Internet Kids" invites viewers to make their own home page, visit the Kremlin, look inside the human heart, take Socks special VIP tour of the White House, and make a boat trip around the world http://www.well.com/user/polly/ikyp.exp.html.

✦ Berit's "Best Sites for Children" help you learn about earthquakes, visit the imagination factory and make junk mail jewelry, descend into a volcano, tour a human cell, go on a world "surfari," solve a crime, and fly a kite http://db.cochran.com/dbHtml:thepage.db.

✦ Steve Savitzky's "Interesting Places for Kids" is an award-winning site in its own right with many unusual links http://www.crc.ricoh.com/people/steve/kids.html.

Online Reference Material

✦ The American Academy of Pediatrics' http://www.aap.org has a wide variety of information for parents concerning their children's health and well-being; covering topics such as immunizations, sleep problems, newborn care, and television.

✦ The National Urban League http://www.nul.org is a useful resource for tracking programs and events related to African-American issues. It is a rich reference area for students, parents, teachers and history buffs.

✦ AskERIC, a free question-answering service provided by the Educational Resources Information Center (ERIC), invites people to submit their questions about education, parenting, and child development to askeric@askeric.org for an e-mail response within 2 working days.

✦ B.J. Pinchbeck's "Homework Helper" is a wonderful guide to encyclopedias, dictionaries, reference works, and other resources on a great variety of subjects http://tristate.pgh.net/~pinch13/. The enthusiasm of its 10-year-old creator adds appeal to everything from the Ultimate White Pages to Bugs in the News.

✦ "My Virtual Reference Desk" http://www.refdesk.com offers dozens of links—to dictionaries, encyclopedias, reference/research materials, thesauruses, atlases, sports, entertainment, and much more—as well as a search engine for locating more information.

✦ The "Internet Public Library: Reference Center" http://www.ipl.org/ref provides an "ask a question" feature and a teen collection, as well as sections on reference, arts and humanities, science and technology, and education.

✦ Driver safety information: Check the GEICO online service. http:\\www.GEICO.com

Sites for Parents & Parent Groups

✦ The Children's Partnership http://www.childrenspartnership.org offers, for free, the full text of its useful guide, "The Parents' Guide to the Information Superhighway: Rules and Tools for Families Online," prepared with the National PTA and the National Urban League. A printed version of the guide, which provides common-sense guidance and encouragement for parents and tips and computer activities for children, is available for $8 from The Children's Partnership, 1351 Third Street Promenade, Suite 206, Santa Monica, CA 90401–1321; (310) 260–1220.

✦ The National Parent Information Network http://npin.org cosponsored by the ERIC Clearinghouses on Elementary and Early Childhood Education and Urban Education, includes extensive articles on parenting, listservs, and links to more than 100 sites on education, health and safety, family issues and interests, and parenting and development of children from infancy to adolescence.

✦ At the National PTA site http://pta.org./ learn about PTA education programs and participate in a discussion group, chat room, or bulletin board. The site also includes links to sites of many organizations concerned with children.

✦ The Family Education Network http://www.familyeducation.com offers hundreds of brief articles on parenting, links to sites, and discussion boards that connect parents with online experts.

✦ The Partnership for Family Involvement in Education http://www.ed.gov/PFIE sponsored by the U.S. Department of Education, highlights school-community-business partnerships and includes a calendar of events. At the home page for the Department of

Education http://www.ed.gov, parents will find information about the President's education initiatives, college financial aid, and parenting publications, along with links to other useful education sites.

✦ The National Coalition for Parental Involvement in Education http://www.ncpie.org/ provides a catalog of resources available from all its member organizations.

✦ The National Coalition of Title I/Chapter 1 Parents (202) 547–9286 helps economically disadvantaged parents develop skills to enhance the quality of their children's education.

✦ The Parents at Home site http://advicom.net/~ism/moms, especially for an at-home parents, offers e-mail pen pals, a booklist, & links to children's sites.

✦ Magellan http://www.mckinley.com/magellan uses a rating scale to evaluate parenting sites. To look at the ratings or follow the links, select Reviews, Life & Style, Family, & Parenting.

✦ The ASPIRA Association, Inc. http://www.incacorp.com/aspira highlights its two national parent involvement programs – ASPIRA Parents for Education Excellence Program (APEX) & Teachers, Organizations, & Parents for Students Program (TOPS). Each program provides a Spanish/English curriculum that strives to empower Latino parents & families.

✦ The White House http://www.whitehouse.gov/WH/New/Ratings describes a strategy to involve government, industry, parent, & teachers in putting together a rating system so parents can define material they consider offensive & protect their children effectively.

Resources From the National PTA

Planning Kits Guides, and Videos for Parents and Educators

The following are publications available through the National PTA Catalog. For full descriptions of these materials, send your request to National PTA, 135 LaSalle Street, Dept. 1860, Chicago, Illinois 60674-1860 or call (312) 549-3253

Common Sense: Strategies for Raising Alcohol & Drug Free Children (K-102)

Ebony/National PTA Guide to Student Excellence, video and parent guide (V-354)

The Family Nest (El Nido de la Familia), Spanish video with accompanying parent involvement tips in Spanish and English (SV-355)

Mirrors: A Film About Self-Esteem (See catalog for special ordering instructions)

Safeguarding Your Children (VP-150)

Brochures for Parents and Educators

Helping Your Child Become a Good Reader (B-323)

Helping Your Student Get the Most Out of Homework (B-307) (In Spanish S-321)

Make Art a Part of Your Child's World (B-311)

Making Parent-Teacher Conferences Work for Your Student (B-312) In Spanish (S-322)

The Busy Parent's Guide to Involvement in Education

Television and Your Family

Helping Your Child Learn

Join the Partnership for Family/School Involvement in Education

Families and schools across America are increasingly accepting mutual responsibility for children's learning. When families are involved in children's learning, at school and at home, schools work better and students learn more. Schools and families are working with employers and community organizations to develop local partnerships that support a safe school environment where students learn to challenging standards. By working together, exchanging information, sharing decision-making, and collaborating in children's learning, everyone can contribute to the education process.

To join the Partnership for Family Involvement in Education, call (800) USA LEARN for more information or send your name, organization, address, city, state, zip code, telephone, fax and E-mail address to:

Partnership for Family Involvement in Education, 600 Independence Avenue, SW, Washington, DC 20202-8173 or fax to (202) 401-3036.

It's a win-win partnership for everyone involved!

In Support of Parents

The following organizations provide support and services for parents and families with various needs:

Children's Rights Council (CRC) is a Washington, DC based organization that works to strengthen families through education and advocacy. It is concerned with the healthy development of children of divorced and separated parents. CRC works to strengthen families and reduce the trauma of divorce to children through supporting legislation and programs, which favor joint custody (shared parenting), mediation, access (visitation) enforcement and fair child support. With 38 chapters in 30 states, this organization has played a major role in educating policy makers about the importance of Parenting Education. CRC has worked extensively on Welfare Reform with proposals in the areas of (1) Eligibility, (2) Parentage establishment and (3) Kinship Care. CRC also publishes many books and tapes. For a copy of *The Best Parent is Both Parents,* contact them at (202) 547–6227 or toll free (800) 787–KIDS.

Parents Anonymous, Inc. is the nation's oldest and largest child abuse prevention organization dedicated to strengthening families. There are 2,300 Parents Anony-mous groups throughout the United States which meet weekly, are co-led by parents and professionally trained facilitators and are free of charge to participants. These groups provide a safe haven for parents seeking more effective methods of parenting. Through Parents Anonymous' community based groups, parents and children gain self-esteem and effective skills to strengthen their families. For information call the national office, (909) 621-6184.

Join Together Online is a National Resource Center and meeting place for communities working to reduce substance abuse (illicit drugs, excessive alcohol and tobacco) and gun violence. For a free calendar of national events contact them at Join Together, 441 Stuart Street, Boston, MA 02116, tel: (617) 437–1500, E-Mail info@jointogether.org on the web at www.jointogether.org

Parents Without Partners (PWP) provides single parents and their children with an opportunity for enhancing personal growth, self-confidence and sensitivity towards others by offering an environment for support, friendship and the exchange of parenting techniques.

Each chapter is committed to running programs that provide educational activities, family activities and adult social and recreational activities. They also conduct community service programs and outreach such as speakers for seminars and workshops, fundraising for national and local charities and cooperative exchanges. Check your local phone book for the chapter nearest you or call (800) 637–7974.

**APPALACHIA
EDUCATIONAL
LABORATORY**

AEL works closely with schools, school districts, and states to help educators, policy makers, parents, and communities strengthen schools and help students learn. One basic goal lies at the heart of our work—linking the knowledge from research with the wisdom from practice to improve both teaching and learning. We are one of 10 Regional Educational Laboratories across the country supported by the U.S. Department of Education's Office of Educational Research and Improvement.

AEL pioneered work in home-based preschool education 30 years ago. That early work constituted a broad, deep foundation for research-based *Family Connections*, one of AEL's signature programs. These parent-tested, teacher-approved learning guides help families and young children have fun learning together and help schools boost parent involvement. Programs in 46 states have purchased the colorful, user-friendly materials for families to enjoy at home.

Now, for the first time, AEL is making *Family Connections* available to individuals. *Family Connections 1* is for parents with preschool children. It is also available in Spanish as *Relaciones Familiares 1*. Parents with kindergarten children will want *Family Connections 2*.

For more information about the *Family Connections Parent Notebook*, see our ad in this publication, call AEL (800)624-9120, or visit our Web site: http://www.ael.org/rel/fc.

An equal opportunity/affirmative action employer

P. O. Box 1348 ▪ Charleston, WV 25325-1348
(304)347-0400 ▪ (800)624-9120 ▪ (304)347-0487 Fax
aelinfo@ael.org ▪ http://www.ael.org

Hand In Hand

Hand in Hand: Parents-Schools-Communities United for Kids is a national initiative launched by the Mattel Foundation in 1995 to build and strengthen partnerships to improve the education of all children. This $3 million initiative was developed after Mattel commissioned a national parent survey which revealed that regardless of education, race or socio-economic status, educational involvement is a priority for parents. Further, many parents lack information on how to participate in schools or they lack the flexibility at work to volunteer during school hours. Another key finding is the importance of linking home activities with lessons at school.

Hand in Hand shares information about programs that expect, value, and nurture the family and community role in children's learning.

For more information contact: Hand in Hand, c/o Institute for Educational Leadership, 1001 Connecticut Ave., NW Suite 310, Washington, D.C. 20036, (202) 822–8405 ext. 25, (202) 872–4050, Email: hand@iel.org, Website address: www.handinhand.org

National Parents' Day Coalition

The National Parents' Day Coalition (NPDC) is a membership-based organization for parenting professionals, parents, organizations, agencies, churches and faith-based groups.   It is the natural outgrowth of a grassroots coalition that came together in 1994 to support Federal Legislation designating, the fourth Sunday in July as Parents' Day.

The Coalition hosted the first annual awards ceremony on Capitol Hill in July 1994.   It was a celebration about good parenting and the role models who embody that concept.

New York Congressman Floyd Flake, who co-sponsored the House of Representatives resolution affirmed the tremendous influence of parents. "I came from parents who gave birth to 13 children; my parents had fifth and sixth grade educations," Flake told the gathering. "People keep asking me how did you survive? I can't help but rejoice in having parents who understood and, in spite of never having taken a psychology course . . . they nurtured us."

Among those being honored were: actress Phylicia Rashad, who played Claire Huxtable on "The Cosby Show;" Roebuck "Pop" Staples, of the Staple Singers; Harriet Nelson of "The Ozzie & Harriet Show;" Florence Henderson, who played Carol Brady on "The Brady Bunch," actor John Forsythe, who starred in "Bachelor Father;" W.W. Johnson, a community activist; actress Barbara Billingsley, who played   June Cleaver in the series "Leave It to Beaver" and Bill Cosby, who played Cliff Huxtable.

The awards continue annually. The 1998 awards were presented in six categories:

The Clarion Award: The National PTA. In its second century of advocacy, the National Parent Teacher Association sets the standard for effective use of all forms of media to promote responsible parenting and positive family values. Included in the National PTA portfolio are *Our Children Magazine*, *Children First* website, *Voice of the PTA* promotional video, and many print, video, audio and electronic resources.

The Liberty Award: This award is presented to an individual or organization who has assisted in the introduction, passage and support of legislation that improves the quality of life for parents and children. This year's recipients are Senator Dale Bumpers and his wife Betty Bumpers, selected specifically for their work to advance immunization for children.

The Phoenix Award: Family Information Services received the Phoenix Award. This unique professional development program offers practitioners a large array of resources for their work and families. It honors and supports the work of professionals in the field by using guest faculty to write the monthly programs. Family Information Services exemplifies the professionalism in the field and creates public awareness about the need for responsible parenthood.

The Vanguard Award: Ceridian Corporation, based in Minnesota, leads the way in information services and defense electronics as well as modeling progressive workplace policies and programs. They give employees the support they need to effectively balance work and home, which leads to greater productivity and success for Ceridian and the individual families. Ceridian is recognized for its progressive workplace policies and programs benefiting and supporting parents.

The Horizon Award: Each year, NPDC recognizes a student on the horizon. This year the award went to Al Bartell, a student at National Lewis University completing his Masters of Human Resources Management and Development. He also is working with The Carter Collaboration Center in conflict management. His leadership places him at the head of many advisory tables and his ideas are being implemented in the lives of many families.

The Ruth Bowdoin Award: The establishment of this award was announced in July. Mrs. Clemmie Collins of Alabama is the recipient. Dedicated to education, Mrs. Collins has given over thirty years to education in the classroom and in the home. She demonstrates the knowledge, skill and compassion that Ruth Bowdoin models in her outreach to children and their families.

The Awards Ceremony kicks off the Annual **"Strengthening Families-Building Communities Conference and Satellite Broadcast."**

PHOTOGRAPHY

PORTRAITURE
Families
Executives

SPECIAL EVENTS
Weddings
Bar Mitzvahs
Bat Mitzvahs

LOGOS

POSTERS

COMMERCIAL
Products
Interiors
Industrial
Photo Decor

BROCHURES

GRAPHIC

DESIGN

PUBLICATIONS
Design
Layout
Typesetting
Illustration

SAM BROWN
PHOTO/GRAPHICS
(301) 925-9522
1220 Caraway Court, Suite 1030
Largo, MD 20774

"I figure if they saw that I cared enough about what they were doing to help them (my children) achieve their goals, then I could count on their cooperation and input toward my goals as a parent."

Mrs. Delores Jordan
Author, Family First, mother of five
including basketball great, Michael Jordan

Parental Involvement Pledge

As A Parent, I pledge to

- Show my child that I value education;
- Encourage my child to be a reader;
- Talk to my child about his/her schoolwork;
- Visit the school;
- Meet the teachers;
- Learn what the school is doing for my child, and
- Learn how I can take part.

I pledge to get involved and stay involved, for education is key to success, and is the greatest gift I can give my child.

_____
Parent's Signature

_____
Parent's Signature

_____
Student's Signature

_____
Date

notes

notes